JCB

Learning and Teaching in the Early Years

Active learning

A practical guide to how babies and young children learn

by Helen Moylett

Contents

Foreword *by Jennie Lindon*   2

Introduction   3

Chapter 1: What does 'Active learning' mean?   6

Extrinsic motivation   7
Intrinsic motivation   9

Chapter 2: Children being involved and concentrating   17

Schemas   19
Well-being and involvement   20

Chapter 3: Children keeping on trying   27

Persistence   28
Resilience   31

Chapter 4: Children enjoying achieving what they set out to do   37

Mastery and performance goals   41
Rewards and praise   43

Chapter 5: Leading a thoughtful approach   50

Effective leadership   52
Links between the characteristics   53

References   61

Published by Practical Pre-School Books, A Division of MA Education Ltd, St Jude's Church, Dulwich Road, Herne Hill, London, SE24 0PB.

Tel: 020 7738 5454

www.practicalpreschoolbooks.com

© MA Education Ltd 2013

Design: Alison Cutler **fonthill**creative 01722 717043

All images © MA Education Ltd. All photos taken by Lucie Carlier with the exception of pages 2-3 and 17 © Sam Hustler; pages 6, 9-10, 12, 21, 23, 28-29, 37, 41-42, 44, 46 and 49-50 © Homerton Children's Centre.

ISBN 978-1-907241-35-2

Foreword

Focusing on learning and teaching in the early years

Anyone with children's best interests at heart will agree upon the crucial importance of experiences over the earliest years. However, good intentions are not enough to champion young learners. During early childhood, genuinely helpful adult behaviour – 'teaching' – looks very different from the version that suits older children and the classroom environment.

Those adults, who make a real difference, are knowledgeable about child development and committed to a warm relationship with individual children and their families. They are also confident to be led by young children's personal time frames and learning journeys. They pay close attention to the current interests of young girls and boys and their enthusiasm for further discoveries.

The authors of this informative series close the gap of meaning that can exist between familiar phrases and a full understanding of what the words mean in best early years practice. Helen Moylett brings alive the concept of babies, toddlers and young children as active learners. Examples and explanation support readers to notice how young children are keen to persist, when they can make genuine choices in a shared enterprise.

By Jennie Lindon, early years consultant

Introduction

About the series

This book is one of a series of three:

- Playing and exploring

- **Active learning**

- Creating and thinking critically.

The starting point for all three books is that babies and young children are already, from birth, creative and competent thinkers and learners – actively involved in their play and gathering information, ideas and knowledge to build their development and learning.

The youngest babies and children are able to use most of the same strategies that will support them as learners all their lives, such as imitating others, playing with things and finding patterns in their experience so they can predict what will happen. These books unpack how children learn and how adults can best support them in being and becoming learners for life.

Playing and exploring, active learning and **creating and thinking critically** are key characteristics of how children learn and have been linked in recent developmental psychology research to the concept of 'self-regulation'. Self-regulation involves attitudes and dispositions for learning and an ability to be aware of one's own thinking. It also includes managing feelings and behaviour. Self-regulation underpins learning across all areas, developing from birth and supporting lifelong learning (Bronson, 2000).

All babies and young children are different so there is no 'one size fits all' way to foster these characteristics of learning. Young children respond to, and join in with, experiences in different ways depending on a host of factors, including their temperament and the opportunities they have already had. However the essential message of this book, and the others in the series, is that children (and their families) are entitled to

practitioners who are open to learning from the children with whom they work and who:

- Provide emotional warmth and security

- Tune-in to each unique child by observing and interacting sensitively

- Use observation and knowledge of child development to assess where children are in their learning and plan for next steps and challenges.

All three books provide many illustrative case studies and examples of real-life encounters with children's **active learning**, their **play and exploration** and their **creative and critical thinking**. All these examples demonstrate practitioners and children engaged together in supporting and extending children's learning.

The characteristics of children's development and learning were embedded in previous English frameworks and recognised in the commitments, which uphold the principles of the EYFS. The Tickell review (2011) of the EYFS drew on recent research and evidence from practitioners and academics across the early years sector in re-emphasising and highlighting those commitments as the **characteristics of effective learning** and they are an important part of the revised EYFS (2012).

As we look at the three characteristics and the underlying aspects of each one, it is important to remember that they are all interlinked. So imagine that the grid below is like a child's piece of weaving, where they have carefully woven individual strands one way and then another so that they are criss-crossing. This is how it should look and is, in reality, how all children develop and learn.

The three characteristics emphasise **how** babies and young children go about the business of learning, rather than simply focusing on **what** they learn.

How children develop and learn is about the way in which they grow as thinkers and learners and involves them developing learning dispositions such as: curiosity, persistence, concentration, motivation, confidence and excitement. It is about becoming an independent thinker and learner who is able to make decisions and choices and interpret their ideas and solve problems.

Practitioners should find these examples useful in reflecting on their own practice and the early years framework with which they work. The books focus particularly on the English Birth to Five framework: the Early Years Foundation Stage (EYFS), but the characteristics of effective early learning are not tied specifically to any one cultural frame of reference and we hope practitioners working with other frameworks will find the discussion of learning and the ways in which adults support it, transcends national boundaries.

The characteristics of effective learning

Playing and exploring			
Engagement	Finding out and exploring	Playing with what they know	Being willing to 'have a go'
Active learning			
Motivation	Being involved and concentrating	Keeping on trying	Enjoying achieving what they set out to do
Creating and thinking critically			
Thinking	Having their own ideas	Making links	Choosing ways to do things

> "The starting point for all three books is that babies and young children are already, from birth, creative and competent thinkers and learners ~ actively involved in their play and gathering information, ideas and knowledge to build their development and learning."

If children have all these internal 'tools' at their fingertips as well as a good dose of self-confidence, well-being and resilience then **what** they learn will be encountered in a much more meaningful and enjoyable way.

What children learn is about the actual content or knowledge, so, for example, in the EYFS in England this is the **prime** and **specific** areas of learning – although there are many crossovers, particularly between the content of Personal, Social and Emotional Development and the characteristics. All learning is underpinned by social and emotional development. Generally we can see the **what** of children's learning, or the content, as being like the bricks of a building with the **how** children learn and their social and emotional development as the cement and foundations – without which everything would topple over. The rest of this book explains this in much more depth across the age range from babies to children in school.

Just as the characteristics are woven together, so the three books in this series link together.

For example, in Chapter 1, there is a shared case study about Jago as he plays with a box of balls. Each book looks at Jago's experience and learning from the different perspectives of **active learning, playing and exploring** and **creating and thinking critically**.

Throughout all three books there are further case studies, observations, suggestions for supporting children's language development, reflection points and recommended reading.

About this book

Active learning looks in depth at what is meant by active learning for babies and young children. It explores the developmental theory behind this and how it links to good practice. It unpicks each aspect of active learning in terms of what it means and how it can be observed and developed in practice.

Some of the key themes of this book are:

- Why and how children are motivated to learn

- How adults can support children's active learning through being effective role models in positive relationships and enabling environments

- The importance of well-being, resilience and persistence in becoming a self-regulated lifelong learner

- The need for close observation in order to support children with time and space for deep involvement in learning.

Chapter 1: What does 'Active learning' mean?

Active learning is all about **motivation** and is a key characteristic of lifelong learning, closely associated with becoming a self-regulated learner. Self-regulation includes the ability to control one's emotions as well as one's cognitive or learning processes.

Martha Bronson (2003) defines cognitive self-regulation as *'the ability to control attention, to direct and monitor thinking and problem solving and to engage in independent learning activities'*. These abilities alongside the ability to understand and work with our emotions are critical for our lifelong learning.

An active learner, whether nine months or ninety-years-old, is not necessarily physically active and moving her body (although in the case of babies and young children this is very likely) but she is definitely participating mentally and emotionally and, above all, she has a real will to learn – a strong motivation to get involved. Being motivated to learn is not only important in early childhood but also a key indicator of success throughout life. The ways in which adults nurture, support and extend babies and young children's capacity for active learning are therefore crucial for those children's future well-being and achievement.

Theory into practice

Motivation has been described in many ways. Broadly speaking we can say that motivation is the **will to learn**, the driving force that makes us do something – the reason we commit ourselves to being involved in an activity, persist in carrying it out and possibly try again to succeed if our first attempts fail. In this book we are going to be exploring motivation as the central idea underpinning three important and interwoven strands of active learning:

- Being involved and concentrating

- Keeping on trying

- Enjoying achieving what they set out to do.

Each of these strands has a chapter devoted to it where the strand is unpicked in more detail and effective early childhood practice is discussed. This chapter gives an overview of all three and looks at some of the theories which inform current thinking and practice about active learning.

Some big questions for early years practitioners are:

- Where does motivation come from?

- How can we best support and extend it?

Sources of motivation to learn

Over the years a number of theories have been advanced as to how children learn. Many of them continue to influence our thinking about children and our practice in working with them. There are two main schools of thought embedded in the theories we are going to look at now – **social constructivism** and **behaviourism**.

Social contructivism tells us that children are born with the will to learn, beginning from birth to make sense of the world 'from the inside out' in interaction with others – here we say **motivation is intrinsic**. **Behaviourism** assumes that learning comes more from factors external to the child – 'from the outside in' – **motivation is extrinsic**.

So which way of looking at learning is right? The answer is both. Even though many early years academics and educators may seem to frown on behaviourism, in fact most effective early years practice uses some elements of behaviourism alongside large amounts of social constructivism. Our current understanding, and the frameworks with which we work, continue to be informed by these ways of understanding children's learning. Let's look first at extrinsic motivation and behaviourism.

Extrinsic motivation

At its crudest, extrinsic motivation may be seen as **bribery**. For example: "If you put these balls away in the box, I'll give you a sticker." The child learns that the point of the activity is to please the adult and gain the reward, not to feel a sense of responsibility and gain the satisfaction of knowing that the balls are stored safely, ready for next time, or to find out that putting them away can be an enjoyable activity in itself.

This approach is linked to thinking about learning as merely a matter of conditioning the child to act in ways which the adults deem appropriate. Psychologists such as **Pavlov** and **Skinner** developed theories through their practical work and research on animals which have been universally applied to human beings and are often known as **behaviourism**. Pavlov's theory of **classical conditioning** can be seen in action in many situations where we do something in response to a stimulus. In schools, for example, when the bell rings children and staff tidy up and get ready for what they expect comes next – break, lunchtime, home time. If the bell rings at the wrong time they may still tidy – because the bell conditions their behaviour more strongly than their own awareness of time. Their actions are extrinsically motivated.

Skinner's theory of **operant conditioning** takes these ideas further with **positive and negative reinforcement**. If behaving in a certain way leads to a positive outcome, that behaviour will be repeated. Jess who is 14 months, for example, may throw a spider toy onto the floor from her highchair. She points to it and her father picks it up and makes it climb up the side of the highchair while he sings "Incey wincey spider is climbing up the highchair" Jess laughs, squealing excitedly when the spider reaches the tray. She throws it again, and again her father repeats the game. This routine is repeated several times. This is known as positive reinforcement – the reinforcer is the game.

Negative reinforcement is when the child behaves in a certain way to avoid something unpleasant. So, for example, Jess may soon stop wanting to play the toy throwing game because her nappy is soiled and wet and she is feeling uncomfortable. She knows that crying will cause her father to make her feel better. So she cries and, as expected, her father soothes her, lifts her up and takes her to change her nappy. Here the reinforcer is the nappy change.

In both these situations Jess is learning that a particular behaviour will lead to a particular response from her father. As long as he goes on responding in these ways she will repeat the behaviour. If he ignores it, instead of rewarding it, she will eventually stop. This application of positive and negative reinforcers is often known as behaviour modification or behaviour management.

In the example of bribery mentioned earlier, the reward for tidying up is the sticker and it is mentioned before the desired behaviour happens. Punishment may also be mentioned before an action – for example: "If you don't put the balls away in the box, I'll put you on the naughty step." In behaviour management, consistent reinforcement of desirable behaviour and ignoring of undesirable behaviour come only after the behaviour has occurred. They are more effective than bribery and punishment and they may be seen as closer to intrinsic motivation as they respond to the actions of the child.

It is important to be clear that positive and negative reinforcement are ways of managing or modifying behaviour and are not the same as bribery and punishment.

However, there are risks involved in relying only on behaviourism to inform early years practice. It is sometimes difficult, for example, to be sure that as adults we are clear both with ourselves and the children as to what is desired behaviour. Take a very common occurrence in early years settings around the need to share resources. Jordan and Awais are both three-years-old. Awais is bigger and stronger than Jordan. Jordan has a bike that Awais wants. Awais runs over and hits Jordan who gets

off the bike in tears. Both children see Gemma, a practitioner, approaching. Jordan runs to her saying "Awais hit me". Awais peddles quickly away and Gemma calls him back. She frowns and looks at Awais raising her voice as she says: "Awais that was very naughty, you know you shouldn't hit. What do you say?". Awais looks down and without looking at Jordan who is still sobbing, quickly says "Sorry Jordan". Gemma smiles at both children and tells Awais to give the bike back to Jordan who peddles off. Ten minutes later the same scenario happens again.

The children may both have learned that …

- if you are bigger and stronger than someone else you get what you want

- it's ok to take something and hurt someone else in the process as long as you say sorry afterwards – or alternatively do the violent taking when the adult cannot see you.

They may also have learned in other situations in the setting that…

- you only get attention if you are disruptive

- conflict has to be sorted out by an adult.

Because wanting an object that someone else is playing with, and trying to get it, is a common situation, this is probably consolidating and reinforcing earlier learning on the same theme.

- The practitioner has responded to the actions of the children but she has not been clear about behaviour to be reinforced and they have probably learned things she did not intend. The children's learning about some very important social skills has been controlled by the adult – motivation to learn is extrinsic.

- Neither child has been encouraged to be an active learner developing intrinsic motivation through experiencing the satisfaction of cooperating with others, thinking about a problem, or using language to resolve conflict. Things could have been different if the practitioner had been clear about behaviours to be reinforced and had focused on supporting the agency and feelings of those involved. We will come back to how she might have done that later in this chapter.

This reliance on the adult being in sole charge of learning is seen in **transmission models of learning** which in the past have looked at children as 'clay' to be moulded, 'empty vessels' to be filled or 'blank slates' to be inscribed by educators. This means

Pause for thought

- What have Jordan and Awais learned ?

- What behaviour is Gemma, the practitioner, reinforcing?

that children are told or shown by adults what they need to know or do and it is their job to remember and/or practise what needs to be done and carry out the task correctly. In some cases this form of direct instruction is appropriate – as in being shown how to use scissors correctly and safely, for example.

However, if this is the only way children are taught, it does not allow for the freedom to use imagination, to try things out and to take risks by doing something in ways that the adult has not thought of. It takes all responsibility for learning away from the learner and can lead to children feeling no sense of agency or control – only confidently doing something if they know they can 'get it right'.

This approach clearly does not support self-regulation. Those children who find it hardest to second-guess what the adult wants or to conform to the adult's way of thinking, may soon be labelled as failing or naughty. This can lead to many children losing the 'can do' attitude with which they are born and approaching life with 'I can't' as their general attitude. This is known as 'learned helplessness' and can be seen very early in life if children cannot see and feel the effect of their actions on their surroundings. Severely neglected babies, for example, may stop crying because they have learned that nobody will come and help them.

We are all born with an innate need to feel effective and exercise power over aspects of our environment. This need underlies our motivation to learn and is nurtured by our beliefs about ourselves. Bandura's theory of **self efficacy** provides a view of human behaviour in which the beliefs that people have about themselves are critical elements in the exercise of control and personal agency. He claims: "Self-belief does not necessarily ensure success, but self-disbelief assuredly spawns failure".

Carol Dweck's research on **mindset** also explores the concepts of control and agency and shows us how damaging learned helplessness can be. She talks about people with a **fixed mindset** who have learned to be helpless and who believe that life is largely out of their control; that others are more able; that learning new things is hard and that generally they 'can't do it'. This leads to the tendency to give up early and often.

Those with a **growth mindset** on the other hand, enjoy new challenges believing that they can improve their own skills through hard work and persistence and seeing achievements as a process. They tend to keep going until they have succeeded. As Einstein is reputed to have said: 'It's not that I'm so smart, it's just that I stay with problems longer'.

Both Bandura and Dweck illustrate the importance of intrinsic motivation in becoming an effective learner and in feeling good about the process of learning.

Intrinsic motivation

Extrinsic motivation comes from outside us whereas intrinsic motivation comes from within. We have seen in the previous section how relying solely on extrinsic motivation could be damaging. In this section we are going to explore how intrinsic motivation is more effective for learning in the longer term, as well as how it may be combined with aspects of behaviourism or extrinsic motivation to support children's learning.

To summarise some important aspects of current understanding about learning, we now know that:

● Children are competent learners from birth

● Their motivation to learn comes from their innate and strong desires to be connected to others, to make sense of their world and to exert control over it by having agency – the ability to make things happen

● They learn in dynamic interaction with other people and with their environment.

This understanding about children's development and learning can be seen influencing and underpinning many early childhood curriculums. For example the commitments and principles of the Early Years Foundation Stage in England, the Scottish Under Threes guidance and Curriculum for Excellence, the Foundation Phase in Wales, Te Whariki in New Zealand, the Hundred Languages of Children approach of Reggio Emilia in Italy, High Scope in the US and also in the Steiner Waldorf and Montessori approaches to early years education.

All these frameworks, and many others, focus more on the child's learning than the adult's teaching and see children as whole human beings in their own right, as well as people on the road to becoming adult.

Social constructivism is at the heart of this approach. Social constructivism builds on both behaviourism and the opposite of behaviourism – the leave it to nature or 'laissez faire' approach where the adult observes what the child is doing and supports that learning but rarely intervenes to take the learning further.

Social constructivists believe that, although when young children are left to their own devices in a stimulating learning environment most will usually learn through exploration and play, it is through the active intervention, guidance and support of a skilled adult that children make the most progress in their learning.

Social constructivism is based on the ideas of three very well-known developmental psychologists – **Piaget, Vygotsky and Bruner**. The most important contribution of Piaget's work was his emphasis on children's active role in learning. He showed how children at various stages of development engage in making

Links to practice

Abi and Connor are four-years-old. They are building a tower of wooden blocks. They take it in turns to place the blocks. As time goes on they place larger blocks than the structure can support and it falls. This happens several times.

They are joined by Leroy who gathers a few blocks together and starts placing them in a line, while keeping an eye on the tower building. When the tower falls again he says 'You got to start with big at the bottom – look' He then places four large blocks in a square and then all three children start placing smaller ones on top. Leroy occasionally takes blocks he judges unsuitable off and says things like 'put more on this side' 'find one of those long ones'. In the end the tower is about three times as high as Abi and Connor's first efforts. They smile proudly as the practitioner, Nazreen, takes a photo complimenting them on their joint achievement. Then they knock it down and start again.

This time Leroy supervises the beginning of the process, reminding the others about the four large blocks, then another child calls him to come outside and he leaves. Abi and Connor carry on building and although the tower is not quite as stable and tall as previously, they are very pleased with it and run over to tell Nazreen asking her to take another photo.

Pause for thought

- How has Leroy scaffolded Abi and Connor's learning?

- What is the role of the practitioner in this scenario? What might 'complimenting them on their joint achievement look like?

sense of their world and constructing their own understandings but he did not emphasise the importance of social relationships and has been criticised for neglecting to understand both the role of language in learning and the impact of the social contexts in which his research experiments took place. He is therefore known as a constructivist rather than a social constructivist.

Some followers of Piaget believed that his theories reinforced the 'laissez faire' approach and that the practitioner should be merely an observer and facilitator of children's learning. As Whitebread (2003:2) explains: "*It was claimed that whenever teachers attempted to teach children something, they simply deprived the children of the opportunity to discover it for themselves. This view was partly a reaction against the simplistic 'behaviourist' model that children only learnt what they were taught. To some extent however, it can be seen to have thrown the baby out with the bath water. More recent research inspired by the work of Vygotsky has argued that there is a much more central role for the adult, and, indeed, for other children, in the processes of learning.*"

Vygotsky believed that social relationships are at the heart of learning and that the importance of those relationships lies particularly in their ability to extend learning. His most famous theory involved the **zone of proximal development**. This refers to the gap or zone between children's level of actual development (what they can manage with no help from anyone else) and what they can do with the help of a more knowledgeable adult or child (their level of potential development). As Robson (2006: 28) explains: "*The role of this more experienced other person is to guide a child to a more sophisticated solution to a task in order to support the move from regulation by others to self regulation*".

Bruner built on Vygotsky's work describing the role of this more knowledgeable other, whether adult or child, as **'scaffolding'** learning (see **Links to practice** on previous page).

The role of the practitioner in supporting active learning

Practitioners help children to become independent and motivated learners through providing time, space and materials as well as a warm emotional environment. They need to know, respect and value the children and their families – the role of the key person is very important here. The key person knows her children better than anyone else and is the child's safe base from which they explore the setting. All practitioners also need

to be very clear about how children learn and how best to help them make progress. Let's go back to the scenario we looked at earlier with Awais and Jordan and the bike. This time Gemma, the practitioner acts differently.

Both children see Gemma, a practitioner, approaching. Jordan runs to her saying "Awais hit me". Awais peddles quickly away. Gemma bends her knees so she is at Jordan's level, puts her arm round him and gives him a tissue. She says: "You are upset Jordan, let's wipe those eyes and then you can tell me about what's made you so sad".

Jordan wipes his eyes and says: "Awais hit me and took the bike". Gemma says: "Did he ask you if he could have the bike" 'No' says Jordan. Gemma then looks across the garden and says 'Look Awais has gone over there. Let's go and talk to him about this.' She takes Jordan's hand and they walk across to where Awais is. He sees them coming and stops.

Gemma bends down again and says: "Hello Awais, Jordan is sad about what happened with the bike. He says you hit him". Awais looks down and is clearly uncomfortable. Gemma says: "Can you think of another way to get a turn on the bike?". Awais says 'Use words' Gemma smiles and says 'Yes – can you remember what we said at group time yesterday about good words to use? ' Jordan says 'Stop' 'Yes' agrees Gemma 'Stop is a good word to use if someone is doing something unkind. Perhaps you could have tried saying 'Stop' when

Awais hit you...but what could Awais have said to you when he wanted the bike? "Please can I go" volunteers Awais. "Well remembered" says Gemma smiling at both the children. She asked: "Jordan, would you have given the bike to Awais if he had said 'Please can I have a go?'". Jordan nods. "Jordan when Awais hit you how did you feel?". Jordan says nothing just looks at the ground and shrugs. Gemma looks at Awais. "How do you think Jordan felt?" she says. Awais whispers "sad".

'So what shall we do now?' says Gemma. Awais pushes the bike towards Jordan. Gemma says: 'Do you think it would be fair for Jordan to have another go now?' Both children nod. Gemma says 'OK then Jordan you get on the bike. Awais and I will watch you for a little while and then Awais might like to come and ask you for a go using those words – please can I have a go.'

Jordan peddles off looking happy and Gemma says to Awais: 'Well done for remembering those words, Awais, shall we see what Jordan is doing now? Look he is talking to Imran and Jack and now he is going to the petrol station. Shall we walk over there and you can ask him if you can have a go now?'. Awais agrees and asks Jordan who gets off the bike. Awais says 'Thanks'.

This time Gemma is clear about the behaviour she wants to reinforce:

● Using words to resolve conflict

● Recognising and labelling feelings

● Finding ways forward they can use in different situations.

Both children have been encouraged to be active learners, developing intrinsic motivation through experiencing the satisfaction of cooperating with others, thinking about a problem and using language to resolve conflict. Gemma helps them by supporting them to recall and apply the group time discussion about using words.

Notice that Gemma does not:

● Blame Awais

● Call him naughty

● Insist on him saying sorry.

Instead she focuses on the positive – complimenting him on his recall and his attitude to Jordan having a turn. She is also keen to get him to practise the alternative strategy while she is there to support him – scaffolding his learning.

Gemma acknowledges Jordan's upset reaction to being hit and having the bike snatched but doesn't dwell on it, preferring to focus on finding a solution and getting him to interact with Awais with her support. When he gives 'Stop' as the answer to the question about the words that Awais could have used, she acknowledges his contribution and expands on what he said, implying, without labouring the point, that Awais's behaviour was unkind and encouraging Jordan to continue in the conversation.

She provides a commentary to Awais on what Jordan is doing as a way of reinforcing vocabulary and also as a means of showing her interest in the activities of all the children. Gemma also models a calm way of using words and is emotionally and physically available to the children who are treated as partners in learning. She may be their key person (the fact that she knows about the group time discussion implies that she is, but it may be that all groups were having some discussion about using words to help resolve conflict) If she is not, it would be a good idea to share the children's actions and the ways in which she supported their learning with their key person(s).

Learning Playing and Interacting (page 22) explains that the active intervention, guidance and support of a skilled adult:

> "*… does not mean pushing children too far or too fast, but instead meeting children where they are, showing them the next open door, and helping them to walk through it. It means being a partner with children, enjoying with them the power of their curiosity and the thrill of finding out what they can do*" (page 22).

This ability to 'tune-in' to children is part of the cycle of observation, assessment and planning described in this diagram in Early Years Foundation Stage guidance.

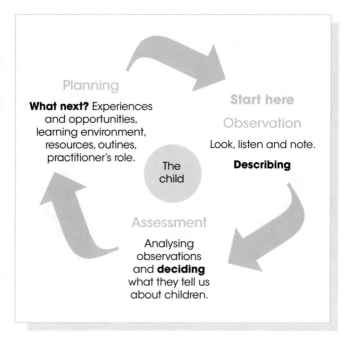

Planning

What next? Experiences and opportunities, learning environment, resources, outines, practitioner's role.

The child

Start here

Observation

Look, listen and note.

Describing

Assessment

Analysing observations and **deciding** what they tell us about children.

We see Gemma putting this cycle into practice in the second bike scenario. First she looks, listens and notes, taking in what has happened. She analyses the information she has and decides that it tells her that Awais needs more practice in asking for what he wants and recognising the feelings of others; that both children need support to use words to resolve conflict and be successful in problem solving and simple negotiations with each other.

She plans some immediate, in the moment, next steps which we see in action and probably also makes a mental note to use this scenario as the basis for some further opportunities to reinforce these (and possibly other) children's learning via a range of activities and group time discussion.

All she does helps the children to develop their intrinsic motivation rather relying on extrinsic motivation – doing things because they want to please an adult or avoid punishment.

Practitioners are not alone in using observation as the basis for future learning. Babies and young children do it too. **Social learning theory** tells us that children learn by imitation as well as by watching others and experimenting in social situations. Bandura, for instance, found that children tend to imitate people in their lives who they feel have status. Parents are clearly very important status figures but so are practitioners, and this should cause us to reflect on what children might imitate.

If, for example, practitioners listen to children, it is likely that they will be good listeners too. If practitioners shout at children, it is likely that children will shout at others. If practitioners are positive and upbeat, it is likely that children will be too. If practitioners explain things to children, the chances are that children will want to explain things too. If practitioners talk about and label feelings children will too. If practitioners are interested in the meaning of words, children will be too.

In terms of active learning it is important that practitioners model behaviours that will help young children have success in each of the three strands of active learning:

- Being involved and concentrating

- Keeping on trying

- Enjoying achieving what they set out to do.

We can see Gemma modelling being involved and concentrating as she focuses on finding a solution that builds on the children's prior learning. She encourages then to keep on trying and to practice alternative solutions and she hopes that they will enjoy achieving something that they set out to do – albeit with a lot of encouragement and positive reinforcement from her.

Most of the children we have seen in the practice examples so far are old enough to be using words but we should not forget that active learning starts from birth, long before we can use words. The final example in this chapter shows all three strands of active learning in action in a young baby's experience with some balls and a box. We can also see how

Case study – Jago and the box of balls

It has been a busy morning at the baby and toddler movement session. An arts centre bar in the evening, the space has been organised creatively by a movement specialist and helper, to allow for safe play and exploration during the day. Jago and his mum are one of the last to leave. Jago's attention is drawn to a shallow cardboard box full of sensory balls. He watches a practitioner put a ball in the box. What he does next illustrates the three strands of active learning:

● Being involved and concentrating
● Keeping on trying and
● Enjoying achieving what he sets out to do.

Jago's face lights up and he crawls swiftly over to the box. He stretches forward, pivoting on one knees with the other leg stretched out for balance. He uses his right and then his left hand to touch the red ball, which is soft and light.

Jago touches and moves the ball with both hands moving the ball back and forth and with a look of real concentration on his face, eventually managing to roll it over the edge.

Jago's motivation comes from within. He is excited to see the ball and needs no encouragement to get **involved and concentrate**.

Links to playing and exploring – finding out and exploring.
Links to creating and thinking critically – having his own ideas.

Active learning
He keeps on trying and concentrates hard on achieving what he sets out to do.

Links to playing and exploring – using what he already knows in his play.
Links to creating and thinking critically – using what he already knows to learn new things.

> "Jago's attention is drawn to a shallow cardboard box full of sensory balls. He watches a practitioner put a ball in the box. What he does next illustrates the three strands of active learning."

The ball rolls away from him across the floor, he immediately turns and crawls quickly after it. He brings the red ball back, crawling, pushing and pinching it between his fingers to move it as he crawls. Then Jago puts the ball back into the box – this takes quite a lot of effort.

He then lifts out one of silver balls, which is solid and shiny. Then another, both balls are then side by side in front of him. He looks very pleased and Natalie, his mother, has moved closer. She tunes in sensing his tiredness and shares his delight by smiling and offering some brief comments .She does not rush him, and waits for him to put the balls back into the box again one at a time. Then she picks him up, cuddles him and they leave

Active learning

When things don't go to plan Jago doesn't get upset. He stays involved with the ball and finds ways to achieve what he sets out to do. Again he concentrates hard, using all his skills.

Links to playing and exploring – being willing to have a go.
Links to creating and thinking critically – having their own ideas, choosing ways to do things.

Active learning

Jago maintains his involvement with the balls in the box. He enjoys his achievement in getting both silver balls out of the box and then back in again. Sensitive adult support scaffolds his learning.

Links to playing and exploring – being willing to have a go.
Links to creating and thinking critically – making links, choosing ways to do things.

the strands of active learning link to the strands of playing and exploring and creativity and critical thinking explored in the companion books in this series.

Jago, like the other children in previous practice examples, and of course many other children, is supported by sensitive and reflective adults.

Many settings offer really good quality provision and staff interactions which support and extend babies and young children's learning. Both Nazreen and Gemma in the examples we have explored are very aware of what, and how, they are trying to teach the children, as well as the words they use and the emotional environment they encourage. They understand that the children's learning processes are supported by communication and language helping them to develop the skills they need to be good thinkers and learners.

Let's think about how Jago communication and language are supported by the practitioner and his mother at his pre-verbal stage.

Communication and language support for Jago

Sensitive adult support – Jago mum communicates her interest by moving closer, sitting still, smiling and watching.

Key words – She offers the occasional word or comment – 'shiny', 'the red ball...' or 'you've got it!' This supports Jago child initiated play and provides simple language to match his experience of 'finding out about balls'.

Reflective practitioner – Imagine yourself when you are trying to learn something new (for example, using an unfamiliar computer to write a report) – too much chat or too many questions can be very distracting and take you away from what you are trying to do.

Enabling environment/mood – Soft music was played from time to time to help create a calm atmosphere during the movement session. At the end, no music is playing and the only sounds are Jago movements and his mother's voice. Babies and young children will benefit from a balance of musical experiences and chat, but too much background noise can inhibit language development (O'Hare, 2006).

Pause for thought

How did Nazreen and Gemma show sensitive support, provide key words and focus on simple conversation and what the children needed to learn?

The next three chapters of this book explore in turn each of the three strands of active learning and what they mean for children and those who work with them. The theme of communication and language will be picked up again in each chapter. In Chapter 2, for instance, we will be looking at what being involved and concentrating looks like and how an awareness of communication and language development helps practitioners understand how best to support children in this aspect of active learning.

> If practitioners explain things to children, the chances are that children will want to explain things too. If practitioners talk about and label feelings children will too. If practitioners are interested in the meaning of words, children will be too.

Chapter 2: Children being involved and concentrating

"The quality of your attention determines the quality of other people's thinking" (Kline, 1999).

Chapter 1 established that active learning is all about motivation and looked at some well-known learning theories and how they relate to motivation.

This chapter explores being involved and concentrating and how practitioners can support and extend babies' and young

children's abilities through the attention they give them, the relationships they establish and the environments they provide.

Why do we become involved?

We get involved in things because we are curious. Sometimes it is fleeting interest where our curiosity is easily satisfied, but at other times our curiosity can become the basis of a much deeper

Links to practice

Chloe and Laura (both three-years-old) are sitting on upturned buckets in the indoor beach.

They are using funnels and buckets to fill containers with dry sand.

Chloe: 'We're making pies'.

Laura *(doesn't look up)***:** 'No but I will later'.

Chloe stays sitting next to Laura but stops playing with the sand and spends some time watching two boys who are shuffling across the floor on their bottoms. She laughs when one rolls sideways when he sees her watching. She says 'Look' to Laura, nudges her and points, but Laura does not look up.

A practitioner is nearby reading a big book with a small group of children. Chloe gets up and goes over, standing on the edge of the group for a minute. The practitioner asks if she would like to come and sit down but she shakes her head and returns to the beach where Laura is still busy with the funnels and containers.

Chloe: 'We're not doing that are we – reading the story?'

Laura *(doesn't look up)***:** 'No we're not.'

She lines up three small buckets and fills them all then she pours the contents of two into a larger bucket. The bucket is almost full. She then picks up small bucket three and hesitates before pouring it slowly into the almost full bucket. The sand begins to overflow but she carries on and fills another small bucket and pours that on as well seeming to enjoy seeing the sand running over the sand in the bucket and onto the ground.

She continues this play for another 10 minutes trying different containers and smiling to herself in anticipation as they near overflowing.

Norland nursery, Bath

involvement. Researchers have studied human curiosity to find out more about how and why we are driven to spend time and energy trying to understand more about other people, places and things.

Nancy Stewart summarising this research, explains that curiosity is initially aroused by noticing something different from what is expected.

> *"This links to an innate explanatory drive, governed by an internal need for consistency with any new information fitting into the understanding we have already constructed – our cognitive map. Something that does not make sense in terms of our existing understanding causes a tension known as cognitive dissonance, and arouses us to try to resolve the inconsistency by seeking more information"* (Stewart, p.54, 2011).

Clearly how much more information we seek will depend to some extent on context, but researchers have also found that two psychological traits work together to sustain deep rather than passing curiosity. These are **openness** and **concern for order**. Sometimes these traits can work against resolving curiosity and dealing with inconsistency. If we are very open, for instance, we may seek lots of new experiences but not necessarily make the effort to think about connections to other learning. If we are very concerned with order we may not want our existing ideas upset and may resist new experiences that challenge our current understanding. Nonetheless, when these two traits come together we can be highly curious people with a strong need for consistency and connection in learning. This willingness to encounter and explore the uncertainty of something new, with the drive to make sense of the experience leads to deep involvement; and deep involvement leads to deeper learning.

Why is concentration so important?

In order to become deeply involved in learning we need to be able to focus on an area of interest for some time in order to investigate and think about it; to concentrate and not get distracted.

> *"An involved child concentrates his/her attention on a specific focus, wants to continue the activity and to persist in it, and is rarely, if ever distracted."* (Pascal and Bertram)

Csikzentmihayli (1979) describes this deep involvement as the state of 'flow', where the experience becomes its own reward. Deep concentration causes feelings of enjoyment and control with no fear of failure and little sense of time.

The Early Years Foundation Stage guidance 'Development Matters' (2012) reminds us that children who are involved and concentrating are likely to be:

- Maintaining focus on their activity for a period of time

- Showing high levels of energy, fascination

- Not easily distracted

- Paying attention to details.

In the case study we can see Laura is so involved in her own investigation that she is able to concentrate all her attention on it. Although she is sometimes aware of Chloe speaking to her and briefly responds, she is not aware of others in the room. Her main focus is her own exploration of the capacity of the containers and she seems to be enjoying that state of flow described by Csikzentmihalyi.

Why is repetition so important for learning?

Anyone who has ever cared for a young child knows that they love repetition. Think about the example of Jess and her father in Chapter 1 – the simple game of dropping the spider from the highchair evoked squeals of delight. So what might Jess be learning?

- Every time I throw the spider it falls (the effect of gravity)

- It is always there on the floor even when you can't see it from the highchair (object permanence)

- Daddy can reach out his hand, pick it up and return it by making it 'climb' (modelling physical skills)

- Daddy always laughs and makes eye contact when the spider falls (appropriate emotional response/bonding with caregiver)

- When we both make eye contact and laugh just before I throw it we are anticipating pleasure together (social communication, making relationships)

- Daddy sings the same song every time and I can hear it's the same even though I don't understand all the words (language and musicality, rhyme, rhythm, intonation).

These repetitions, explorations and experiments are the way children learn. We all need to prove gravity for ourselves rather than be told about it. And in terms of emotional development we need constant repetition of acts of being loved, trusted and given control to begin to understand ourselves and others.

Being able to initiate learning for oneself based on one's own interests is likely to lead to deeper involvement than adult-led activity. If we think again about Laura in the sand, she is in control. At this point in her development the pouring and filling is clearly very important and engrossing.

Chris Athey's work on **schemas** has been influential in helping adults understand the importance of repetition in children's learning. Athey built on the work of Piaget on how children come to construct understanding through experience. Athey defines a schema as:

> "...a pattern of repeatable behaviour into which experiences are assimilated and that are gradually co-ordinated. Co-ordinations lead to higher-level and more powerful schemas" (Athey, p.50, 2007).

On page 20 are some common patterns of behaviour seen in many children. If you are aware of schemas when you observe children you may see these sorts of behaviours repeated regularly. It is important to remember that children may be working with more than one schema at a time, and that if you

Common patterns of behaviour

Schema	Possible behaviour
Trajectory	Throwing items in various directions, climbing up and jumping off
Enveloping	Wrapping self in a blanket, covering whole painting with one colour, putting notes in envelopes to post
Enclosure	Filling and emptying containers, climbing into boxes, making dens
Transporting	Carrying small items round in bags and buckets, pushing other children and objects round in prams and pushchairs
Rotation	Rolling and being spun round, playing with wheeled toys, watching the washing machine
Connection	Joining furniture with wool or ribbon, joining train tracks together, sticking boxes and models together
Positioning	Lining up objects, walking round the edge of things, being particular about where food goes on their plate

want to plan for children based on their schemas you should observe involved behaviour regularly – fleeting interests are not schemas. So, as in this example on page 18, Laura may well be exhibiting aspects of an enclosure schema, but Chloe is not.

Whatever conclusions one draws from the observation of Laura and Chloe, they are both content and enabled to follow their own interests. No practitioner comes along and asks what they are doing or tells them to be careful. They are free to follow their own paths. We will come back to the role of the adult in both being pro-active and hanging back where appropriate, but first let's reflect on the role of well-being in active learning.

Dispositions to learn – well-being and involvement

Dispositions can be broadly defined as **habits of mind**.

> *"Unlike an item of knowledge or a skill, a disposition is not an end state to be mastered once and for all. It is a trend or consistent pattern of behaviour..."* (Katz, p.103, 1995).

Being involved is one of the five domains of **learning disposition** described by Margaret Carr (2001). She describes dispositions as a combination of motivation and learning strategies. These dispositions are an integral part of the 'Learning Story' approach to observation, assessment

and planning developed in New Zealand and are related to the strands of the New Zealand early years curriculum, Te Whariki. All the strands of Te Whariki are interwoven but it is significant that being involved is particularly related to the well-being strand; involvement is what practitioners look for when children are feeling a sense of well-being.

This combination of well-being and involvement as an important indicator of children's learning has also been developed by Ferre Laevers at Leuven university in Belgium and extensively used by Chris Pascal and Tony Bertram in the UK as part of the Effective Early Learning (EEL) and Baby Effective Early Learning (BEEL) programmes.

Laevers (2000) explains why, if we truly we want to assess how children are developing and learning, we should consider these two important aspects.

> *"....we first have to explore the degree in which children do feel at ease, act spontaneously, show vitality and self-confidence. All this indicates that their emotional well-being is o.k. and that their physical needs, the need for tenderness and affection, the need for safety and clarity, the need for social recognition, the need to feel competent and the need for meaning in life and moral value are satisfied.*

> *The second criterion – involvement – is linked to the developmental process and urges the adult to set up a*

challenging environment favouring concentrated, intrinsically motivated activity. Care settings and schools have to succeed on both tasks: only paying attention to emotional wellbeing and a positive climate is not enough, while efforts to enhance involvement will only have an impact if children and students feel at home and are free from emotional constraints".

The Leuven Involvement Scale (LIS) uses five levels as a framework for observing children's involvement:

- **Level 1:** No activity. The child is mentally absent. If we can see some action it is a purely stereotypic repetition of very elementary movements.

- **Level 2:** Actions with many interruptions (e.g. staring into space, fiddling) for approximately half the time of the observation.

- **Level 3:** More or less continuous activity. The child is doing something (e.g. listening to a story, making something with clay, interacting with others, reading, finishing a task). But we miss concentration, motivation and pleasure in the activity. In many cases the child is functioning at a routine level.

- **Level 4:** Activity with intense moments. The activity matters to the child and involvement is expressed for as much as half the observation time.

> **Being able to initiate learning for oneself based on one's own interests is likely to lead to deeper involvement than adult-led activity.**

- **Level 5:** Sustained intense activity. Child's eyes more or less uninterruptedly focused on the activity. Surrounding stimuli barely reach the child and actions require mental effort. Any disturbance or interruption experienced as a frustrating rupture of a smoothly running activity (adapted from Laevers 1994 and Robson 2006).

Theory into practice

Think about the observations below and decide which level of involvement each child seems to be functioning at according to the Leuven Involvement Scale.

- Ruby is five months and not yet crawling. She is lying on her front on a quilt on the floor. She notices a toy that is a few centimetres out of her reach. She focuses her eyes intensely on it with her head raised and stretches her whole body working her legs, arms and hands as she tries to move nearer. She rests now and again but remains focused. Twice she just touches the toy and bats it slightly further out of reach but her gaze remains on it and the process of stretching, wriggling and reaching continues. Finally she grasps the toy securely and brings it straight to her mouth to explore. The whole process takes over three minutes.

- Jamal is three-years-old. He is standing at a table at his pre-school. There are five inset jigsaws on the table. Amy is concentrating on trying to complete one of them. Jamal tips the pieces out of the others, mixes them all up all and then completes all four in less than a minute, whilst singing to himself and glancing up at regular intervals. He continues to stand at the table watching Amy and looking round until a practitioner goes to the outside door, then he runs to his peg and puts his coat on.

- Kai-Lin is two and helping Simon, her key person, lay the table for lunch at nursery. Simon hands her a plate and says 'One for Jaycee', She takes it and puts it next to a beaker. She returns to Simon and he hands her another plate saying one for 'One for Ryan'. She does the same with that and the next one, saying the names after Simon each time. She looks happy and twice says 'Me helpin' and 'Lunch soon'. As she is placing the fourth plate on the table she hears a group of children singing nearby and begins to walk away with the plate in her hand. Simon says 'Kai-Lin' when she turns round he asks with a smile 'Where are you going?' She points to the singers and carries on. Simon watches her. Two minutes later she comes back still carrying the plate and puts it on the table next to a beaker.

- Jordan is in reception class. He is sitting at a table with a worksheet in front of him. The task is to look at each black and white image down the left hand side of the sheet, decide on the word it represents, identify the initial sound of the word and then draw a line linking the image to the letter on the left hand side matching that initial sound. There are six images and six letters. Jordan was given the sheet ten minutes ago when he was sitting on the carpet. It took him three minutes to get to the table as he stopped to talk to his friend Jake on the way and then loitered near another table where children were playing a maths game. Since sitting down with the four other children in the group he has joined up two of the images and the letters. He has

also chatted to the boy and girl sitting on either side of him and they have discussed what they are going to be doing outside at playtime.

There is a table on page 26, at the end of the chapter, which matches the observations of the children with the Leuven Scale.

The role of the adult: Positive relationships and enabling environments

Adults – both parents and practitioners can do many things to support and extend children's involvement and concentration. Sometimes they are more supportive by deliberately not doing anything, apart from observing.

There is no adult involved with Ruby in the example on page 21, in the sense that nobody is talking to her, moving things around for her or showing her how to reach the toy. However the adult (in this case her mother) has played a crucial role in ensuring that she is not interrupted in her struggle to reach out and grasp. (If you want to see Ruby in action go to http://www.janetlansbury. com/2012/05/dont-help-this-baby/.) Ruby's motivation was intrinsic (see Chapter 1) She did not need anyone to urge or tell her she was a good girl and the reward was getting the toy to her mouth to explore. She did not look round for praise.

Sometimes the adult might only observe like Ruby's mother did or sometimes they might offer very minimal support to sustain involvement. This is the sort of support Jago's mother offered him in the example at the end of Chapter 1. She moved closer as she sensed he was tired, smiled, commented briefly and then left him to finish the process, not rushing him and not putting the balls back in the box for him.

The way in which we observe helps us tune in to children as people in their own right who have unique ways of being and doing. It also helps us build positive relationships with them, so that if they asked these fundamental questions the answers are positive.

- Do you know me?

- Can I trust you?

- Do you hear me?

- Is this place fair for us?

● Do you let me fly?

Adapted from Podmore, May & Carr (2001).

If we think about Kai-Lin we see Simon is supporting her with beginning to understand the actions involved in laying the table, one to one correspondence through matching plates to beakers, as well as helping her remember the other children in their group and practise her spoken language skills by saying their names. When he wants her attention he says her name first. He does not stop her wandering off but watches her to find out about her interest in the singing which turns out to be fleeting. He doesn't try and stop her or get into confrontation, but is led by her and waits to see how things will go before deciding what to do about laying the table. The answers to those questions seem to be 'Yes' for Kai-Lin.

If we have positive relationships we will be able to ensure that children develop that crucial sense of well-being that goes hand in hand with involvement and also that what we provide meets the needs of the children. The special relationship that a practitioner has with each child in their key person group should support cognitive development and thinking as well as the child's personal, social and emotional learning.

The best way to improve anyone's thinking is to listen to them with respect and full attention. 'When you are listening to someone much of the quality of what you are hearing is your effect on

them.' (Kline, 1999: 37) This attentive listening often starts with interactions with parents but think about the experience of the children as well as their mother in these two scenarios below.

It might seem that not a lot happens in these short interactions but there are plenty of messages being conveyed which illustrate Kline's point that what we hear from others is often

Thinking about the messages we give parents and children

Setting A has a lovely new building, with a purpose-built shelter for buggies outside the front door. It has a big sign outside in several community languages, and glass doors through which can be seen a spacious entrance area with comfy seating. Emilija, who has only recently arrived in Britain, walks nervously through the gate with her ten-month-old baby and her three-year-old son. She meets a woman outside who is hurrying out of the building and does not introduce herself, but points at the buggy park and says brusquely over her shoulder, 'Leave your buggy in there, we don't want a load of mud on the carpet.' Emilija does not understand all the words but hears the tone, gets the gist and obeys the instruction. She rings the bell with trepidation.

Setting B is a pack-away setting based in a church hall. There is an old easel outside with a plastic covered sign saying 'Welcome' and the setting name in English. Emilija hesitates as she closes the gate, wondering where the door is. Just then a woman hurries round the side of the building. She sees Emilija and her children and her face lights up with a smile. 'Hello,' she says and holds out her hand. 'I'm Lesley.' After a minute's conversation Lesley has found out that Emilija speaks a little English, that she comes from Lithuania, that her son, Dane, has a lovely shy smile and that the baby, Anya, has a cold. She walks back round the building with them and takes them in to introduce them to the manager and carry on the process of getting to know the setting.

From Moylett, H (2011)

Setting B	Setting A
You are welcome	You are not really welcome despite our signs and facilities
You are important to us, we'd like to get to know you	The most important thing is not to get mud on our nice new carpet
We can communicate with each other, we will listen and help you with your English	We tell you what to do
We like children and adults here	We want you to obey the rules
We are kind and friendly	You have got to obey the rule before you are allowed in to find out whether anyone inside the building might be kind and friendly
We don't leave our friendly professional attitudes inside the setting we carry them out into our community	We are not aware of the community outside the setting

our effect on them. The practitioners involved might not have been conscious of it, but above are some the messages Emilija, Dane and Anya were getting.

In setting B the practitioner may have been in a hurry, but she made a few minutes available to establish the beginnings of a positive relationship through paying attention. Imagine how unworried and positive Emilija will be about setting B later on when they are at home and how likely it is that her positive attitude will be shared by Dane.

We know that a warm emotional climate is very important and underpins learning, but it is not enough if we are to be effective early years professionals. Practitioners need to **practise attentive listening** when they are thinking about learning and establishing the right conditions for children to get involved and concentrate.

Development Matters (2012) suggests that adults could provide the following in an enabling environment for active learning:

- Children will become more deeply involved when you provide something that is new and unusual for them to explore, especially when it is linked to their interests.

- Notice what arouses children's curiosity, looking for signs of deep involvement to identify learning that is intrinsically motivated.

- Ensure children have time and freedom to become deeply involved in activities.

- Children can maintain focus on things that interest them over a period of time. Help them to keep ideas in mind by talking over photographs of their previous activities.

- Keep significant activities out instead of routinely tidying them away.

- Make space and time for all children to contribute.

Your ability to listen, the relationships you establish and the things you provide will all contribute to the 'feel' of the place. If we want children to be really involved and concentrate and be motivated and active in their learning early years practitioners have to be fascinated by learning themselves. Dowling (2010:119) suggests that in an effective setting you can tell that people are 'in love' with ideas.

Kline's work has led her to the unsurprising conclusion that, throughout life, the best conditions for thinking are:

- Gentle

- Quiet

- Unrushed

● Stimulating but not competitive.

No setting could, or should, be quiet all the time, but many early years settings are rarely quiet. If practitioners do not ensure, by the way they model it themselves, that getting involved sometimes requires quiet and concentration then children are less likely to develop their own abilities in this area. Practitioners who really pay attention to children and their involvements will not force children to be interested in anything but will gently encourage many different interests and let children lead their own learning.

Pause for thought

● With babies and toddlers do you provide sessions where they can play freely and explore open ended resources eg treasure baskets and/or collections of objects including natural materials?

● Do you really watch with attention where their gaze is going and do you think about how often you might assume what babies want and encourage helplessness rather than control?

● How often do the children in your key group see you getting involved in something interesting?

● Does learning get taken where the children want it to go or do you often stop them if they go 'off message'? (e.g. Kai-Lin laying the table)

● Do routines flow with the children, or do they have to fit in to organisational constraints better suited to adults? Do you change all the nappies at the same time, for example? If you are in a nursery or reception class at school, for instance, are you still following the bells and timetable of the rest of the establishment?

● Do you use the language of involvement with older children? (e.g. 'I was very interested in what you were all learning this afternoon. I was watching Laura in the sand, she was really concentrating on filling buckets.' 'I could see Jayden was thinking really hard about the spider Alice found earlier because he was looking for some books about spiders.')

Chloe and Laura responded differently to the sand because they are unique children. We know that sand is a great learning material but perhaps Chloe was more concerned to be with Laura than engage in exploration. Perhaps she did not need to do all the pouring and filling because she had already had those experiences and did not find them as fascinating. We do not know, but we do know that neither child was made to go in the sand or felt constrained to do any particular activity in it. Despite that, there had been a significant amount of planning by the practitioners who provided the beach in response to many children's interests.

Early persistence

Einstein, who knew a thing or two about involvement and concentration, seemed to decry his own achievements when he said: "I have no special talents. I am only passionately curious". It was that curiosity that kept him working at the theory of relativity for years, despite many setbacks. Most of us will not discover such ground breaking concepts, but if we are encouraged to concentrate and be persistent it will stand us in good stead for the rest of our lives according to some recent research which interestingly compares the long term effects of early persistence with the long term effects of reading and maths ability.

The study followed 430 children from preschool age to adulthood. Parents were asked a series of questions about their child's ability to pay attention at the age of four, such

Pause for thought

● How often do you have a quiet time with children, when you say things like 'Let's think about this, I'm not sure what we're going to do about it'.

● When you are a reading or telling a story do you ever encourage the children to close their eyes and 'see' what is happening in their minds?

● Which areas of your setting do you enjoy being in most? How might this affect your key children's dispositions to learn?

as whether they played with a single toy for long periods and whether they give up easily when confronted by a problem.

Each child's reading and maths ability was tested at age seven and again at age 21.

Contrary to researchers' expectations, they found that maths and reading ability did not have a significant effect on whether or not students gained a university degree. But those who could concentrate and persist at the age of four were almost 50 per cent more likely to have completed a degree course by the age of 25. Dr Megan McClelland, who led the study, said:

> *"The important factor was being able to focus and persist. Someone can be brilliant, but that doesn't necessarily mean they can focus when they need to and finish a task or job...Academic ability carries you a long way, but these other skills are also important ... the ability to listen, pay attention and complete important tasks is crucial for success later in life."*

In the next chapter we will look in more detail at persistence and what is involved in being sufficiently motivated to keep on trying.

Below are children's activity matched to the Leuven involvement Scales.

Below are the observations of Ruby, Jamal, Kai-Lin and Jordan (page 21 and 22) matched to the Leuven involvement Scale.

It is important to be aware that this table only addresses the children's involvement in the task that the adult is expecting them to be doing. Jamal may be functioning at a routine level but consider how aware he is of the setting routine, the actions of practitioners, the need to appear to be busy and a vantage point from which to observe the door. He is organised for getting outdoors as soon as possible! And what about Jordan who is clearly not focused on the worksheet but has been very sociable and skilled at using his journey to his table to interact with a friend, be curious about other activities and, once sitting down, has planned his outdoor activity in advance. Perhaps by 'wasting' worksheet completion time he has managed to ensure that no time will be wasted once outside. Jamal and Jordan have skills that may be missed if we only focus on our expectations rather than the children's actual skills.

Leuven involvement examples

Child	Level of Involvement
Jordan is four and in reception class. He is sitting at a table with a worksheet in front of him.	**Level 2** Actions with many interruptions for approximately half the time of the observation
Jamal is three-years-old. He is standing at a table at his pre-school	**Level 3** More or less continuous activity. The child is doing something but we miss concentration, motivation and pleasure in the activity. In many cases the child is functioning at a routine level.
Kai-Lin is two and helping Simon, her key person, lay the table for lunch.	**Level 4** Activity with intense moments. The activity matters to the child and involvement is expressed for as much as half the observation time.
Ruby is 5 months and not yet crawling. She is lying on her front on a quilt on the floor.	**Level 5** Sustained intense activity. Child's eyes more or less uninterruptedly focused on the activity. Surrounding stimuli barely reach the child and actions require mental effort.

Chapter 3: Children keeping on trying

Persistence is important – messages from research

The research mentioned at the end of Chapter 2 pointed to the lifetime effects of being an active learner who is able to concentrate and persist (keep on trying) in the early years. This confirms the findings of the research associated with the **High Scope** Perry Pre-School project – one of the strongest sources of evidence we have about the long lasting effects of how we are encouraged to learn when we are young. The heart of the High Scope approach is social constructivist (see Chapter 1) supporting children to plan, carry out and review their own learning, motivated by their own ideas and interests and supported by skilled practitioners as appropriate. The original High Scope project has been the subject of a rigorous longitudinal study following children who took part in the

Since 1997 in the UK the **Effective Provision of Pre-School Education (EPPE)** Project has been looking at the effects of good quality early years education and is now following the original children as they finish compulsory education at 16. Like High Scope, the researchers have found that pre-school quality was still predicting better social-behavioural outcomes at age 14.

Both High Scope and EPPE focused on children in provision for three to four-year-olds. Other studies have linked **babies' persistence** at various ages with parenting style and toddler outcomes. For example, one study compared babies' persistence at 6 and 14 months with their mothers' 'teaching style'. They found that mothers who provide access to stimulating objects, are sensitive and responsive to children's emotions and support children's behaviours just above their current level may foster both persistent behaviour and advanced cognitive development in the future. They suggest that practitioners should work with at risk children and families to develop strategies that support the development of persistence as early as possible (Banerjee and Tamis-LeMonda, 2007).

programme until they were over 40-years-old. One strand of the research compared children who had been in the project with those who went to traditional nursery schools (largely child-initiated activity) and those who attended 'direct instruction' (behaviourist/formal, practitioner led) pre-schools.

Children who had attended 'direct instruction' settings showed early achievement gains in English and Maths but as the children got older that advantage disappeared and the balance shifted. By the age of 15 children from the direct instruction group were half as likely to read books, twice as likely to have committed 'delinquent acts' and were far more likely to be socially and emotionally troubled than children from High Scope and traditional nursery schools. By the age of 23 the direct instruction group were almost four times more likely to have been arrested and had almost eight times the rate of emotional impairments. They were about half as likely to have graduated from college.

When, at age 40, the High Scope group were compared with children who did not go to any pre-school provision it was found that they exhibited less anti-social and criminal behaviour and were less likely to be drug-users. They were far more likely to be doing voluntary work in the community, have stable marriages and higher earnings. It is significant that these High Scope children were all born in poverty and had been identified as at risk of academic failure.

The big message from all this research is that what practitioners do in the early years matters for life. As individuals we cannot stop children being born into poverty and disadvantage, but our practice can improve their long-term outcomes. The formal behaviourist view that all learning is shaped by the teacher (as in the direct instruction pre-schools) does not have long term impact on aspects of life which help us sustain our learning, loving and earning power. Concentrating in the early years on how children learn by supporting their well-being and learning strategies, enables them to be more self-reliant active learners who can exercise control over their own lives. If we concentrate on **what** rather than **how children learn**, any short-term gain soon wears off and these children are then left with insufficient emotional and cognitive self–regulation resources to manage their lives successfully. It was the concentration on **how** we learn that ensured the High Scope children were more likely to go to college, rather than filling them up with knowledge that is soon forgotten.

Why keep on trying?

The short answer to that question is because we're born to try. 'If at first you don't succeed, try, try, try again' is an old saying and babies practise it all the time.

"Infants stretch their skills daily. Not just ordinary skills, but the most difficult tasks of a lifetime, like learning to walk and

talk. Babies don't worry about making mistakes or humiliating themselves. They never decide it's too hard or not worth the effort. They walk, they fall, they get up. They just barge forward" (Dweck, 2006, p.16).

Carol Dweck asks 'What could put an end to this exuberant learning?'. The answer from her research is the fixed mindset mentioned in Chapter 1. People with a fixed mindset have a can't do attitude believing that life is largely out of their control, that learning new things is too hard for them, other people are more able. Whereas those with a growth mindset (sometimes called a mastery orientation – see Chapter 4) continue to have an approach to life more like the baby's – enjoying new challenges and believing they can improve their skills through keeping on trying.

Of course babies' initial approach to life outside the womb is largely based on instinct and the need for survival, but it also comes from inborn psychological desires:

● To be competent and make sense of experience

● To have control

● To connect with others.

Even before birth, babies respond to feedback from other people. Within minutes of birth, if all has gone well, they make eye contact and show a preference for relating to people rather than objects. (Murray and Andrews, 2000) It is their caregivers' responses to these early attempts to connect that will be crucial over their next few years in shaping how young children think about themselves as learners and whether they continue to try, try and try again.

Theory into practice

Finn is 12-months-old. He has dropped a small toy into his mother's wellington boot. He tries to retrieve it but his arm is too short to reach to the bottom of the welly. He turns to his mother making sounds of distress. She says gently 'Can you get it?' and he returns to the task.

Maria is four. She has just started in reception class. She wants to go outside and brings her coat to Penny, the teaching assistant who says: 'Are you going to put that on Maria ?'. Maria says 'I can't'. Penny smiles and says 'I bet you can, shall I help you get started?' Maria nods 'Right – the first magic trick is to put the hood on your head.' Maria does this, smiles and says 'I've got a cape' and swirls the coat round. It falls off, but she picks it up and puts it back on her head, looking at Penny expectantly. 'Now, which arm would you like to put in first' says Penny.

● Do you think Finn will be able to put his coat on by the time he is four?

- Why do you think Maria thinks she cannot put her own coat on?

- Can you think of children you work with who give up easily or don't attempt something they think will be challenging?

- Do you ever collude with their lack of persistence by doing things for them before they need or want you to?

- Is there enough time in your daily routines for children to keep on trying?

- What strategies do you have in place to encourage more persistence?

Attachment and brain development

Children like Maria and Finn have obviously been parented in different ways and probably experienced different levels of encouragement to keep on trying. Our earliest experiences are translated into patterns of response in the brain that then determine how we feel about ourselves and relate to others for the rest of our lives.

When babies work out that they can depend on and trust a caregiver (usually, but not always, their mother) who is consistently responsive and sensitive to their physical and emotional needs they have what is called a 'secure attachment'. Babies can also form close bonds with a small group of other people who know them well. These relationships are vital to their learning and development and explain why the key person role in settings is so important.

As babies, we need and seek constant repetition of acts of being loved, trusted and given control to begin to understand ourselves and others. The most fundamental task of a baby is to learn how to meet her needs. When her signals are recognised and she receives what is often referred to as a 'contingent' response based on what she actually needs, rather than on what the carer thinks she might or should need, she will calm, feel secure and begin to be able to regulate her own behaviour.

These early childhood experiences physically determine how the brain is 'wired.' At birth, babies have all, or most, of the brain cells they will ever have, but connections between these cells is incomplete, early experiences wire the connections. Repetition of experiences strengthens them. The first three years see the most rapid changes and this is when the brain is most flexible and prepared to learn. The number of connections can go up or down by 25% or more, depending on the environment. Connections that aren't used are pruned. This can have serious consequences – see diagram below.

Caregiver

Responds predictably and consistently to meet baby's needs e.g. recognises baby's hungry cry, comforts and feeds as quickly as possible, smiles and talks gently making eye contact.

Baby

Soon calms and enjoys feeding;
Distress soon forgotten;
Attention focused on exploring, allowing brain to develop.

Caregiver

Unpredictable and inconsistent and usually does not meet needs e.g. does not attend to baby's cries, leaves to cry, does not have bottles ready, does not smile or talk.

Baby

Remains distressed with energy focused on trying to satisfy need for food;
More difficulty interacting with people and objects due to high stress;
Brain shuts out stimulation needed for learning and development.

- Can you think of children who respond to stress by being very distressed or aggressive?

- What does the behaviour of these four-year-olds tell you about their responses to stress?

Matthew is pretending to be a monster. He has perfected the art of creeping up on other children from behind and scaring them with a loud roar. First he startles Jay who screams, starts crying and runs to the practitioner, who takes several minutes to calm him. Next he comes up behind Kadisha and roars. She jumps and then turning round hits him on the head and shoves him roughly away. When he roars at Alice she screams and then laughs, saying: 'Matthew that was scary'.

As Sue Gerhardt says in the aptly titled *Why Love Matters* (2004):

"Unfortunately, leaving a baby to cry or cope by himself for a very short period usually has the reverse effect: it undermines the baby's confidence in the parent and in the world, leaving him more dependent not less. In the absence of the regulatory partner, a baby can do very little to regulate himself or herself other than to cry louder or to withdraw mentally".

As Gerhardt goes on to point out, these two options are based on primitive responses, which seem built into our human genetic make-up: fight or flight (cry louder or withdraw). Babies learn to self-regulate by repeated experiences of being rescued by others.

When a baby is exposed for too long or too often to stressful situations such as being left to cry, it has physical as well as emotional consequences; her brain becomes flooded with the stress hormone cortisol which is secreted in higher levels during the body's 'fight or flight' response to stress. High levels of cortisol can cause brain cells to die and reduce the connections between the cells in certain areas of the brain, harming the vital brain circuits. Babies with strong, positive emotional bonds with their caregivers show consistently lower levels of cortisol in their brains and develop the ability to regulate their response to stress appropriately.

Resilience

One sign of our developing ability to cope with stress is our resilience. **Resilience** is our ability to bounce back from setbacks. **Attachment** is in large part the elastic that helps us bounce.

Grotberg (1995) defines resilience as 'a universal capacity which allows a person, group or community to prevent, minimize or overcome the damaging effects of adversity.' Clearly many children throughout the world live with all sorts of very damaging adversity like war, poverty and famine. But, on an everyday level, everyone faces setbacks; nobody is exempt. We all need resources on which to draw whether we face natural disaster or we're three and somebody has just scared us. Grotberg through her work with children and parents across the world, identifies three sources of resilience – **I have**, **I am** and **I can**.

I have

- People around me I trust and who love me, no matter what

- People who set limits for me so I know when to stop before there is danger or trouble

- People who show me how to do things right by the way they do things

- People who want me to learn to do things on my own

- People who help me when I am sick, in danger or need to learn.

I am

- A person people can like and love

- Glad to do nice things for others and show my concern

- Respectful of myself and others

- Willing to be responsible for what I do

- Sure things will be all right.

I can

- Talk to others about things that frighten me or bother me

- Find ways to solve problems that I face

- Control myself when I feel like doing something not right or dangerous

- Figure out when it is a good time to talk to someone or to take action

- Find someone to help me when I need it.

She goes on to explain that:

"A resilient child does not need all of these features to be resilient, but one is not enough. A child may be loved (I HAVE), but if he or she has no inner strength (I AM) or social, interpersonal skills (I CAN), there can be no resilience. A child may have a great deal of self-esteem (I AM), but if he or she does not know how to communicate with others or solve problems (I CAN), and has no one to help him or her (I HAVE), the child is not resilient. A child may be very verbal and speak well (I CAN), but if he or she has no empathy (I AM) or does not learn from role models (I HAVE), there is no resilience. Resilience results from a combination of these features".

Theory into practice

Let's apply this framework to a situation where learning is hard for children and they need to be able to bounce back and keep on trying.

Chris is a childminder. She is at home with Oscar, a ten-month-old baby and Lola, a three-year-old. Lola is building a tower out of small wooden blocks. She is totally absorbed in the process, carefully selecting the blocks she wants and rejecting others, she looks at the tower as it progresses and sometimes talks to herself under her breath about what she is doing. Oscar crawls across the room towards her. Chris watches him stop and then reach out, knocking down most of the tower. Lola is startled and pushes the baby roughly away before starting to cry. Oscar also starts to cry.

Chris goes over, sits on the floor and picks up Oscar and at the same time puts her arm round Lola. (She is giving both children the message that she is there for them – **I have**)

They both calm quickly. She says to Lola: "I saw you working very hard to make your tower and you were surprised and upset when Oscar broke it weren't you..?". Lola nods looking sad. Chris adds: "I think Oscar liked your tower too, but he doesn't know how to be gentle yet and you know he likes to knock things down". Chris strokes Oscar's head, saying: "Oscar, you were sad too weren't you when Lola pushed you". Lola reaches over and strokes his head too saying "Sorry Oscar", Oscar smiles at her (The children both feel loved and lovable and Lola shows her concern for Oscar – **I am**).

"Now" says Chris: "Let's think about what we can do to make sure nobody carries on being sad". She pauses and looks at Lola who says: "Oscar can go away, cos he'll do it again, he's little". She kisses Oscar who responds by babbling excitedly. "Yes, he could," says Chris: "I could take him in the kitchen with me and give him some of those pots and pans he loves and I can keep an eye on you from there and watch you rebuilding your tower. We'll close the gate and then he can't crawl away when I'm not looking" (Lola feels consulted about a solution to the problem, she knows she has someone to help her, Chris is helping Oscar to enjoy and pursue his own interests – **I can**).

Notice that neither child was told they were naughty and both are being helped to develop resilience and to recognise that strong feelings are recognised and acknowledged and that adults will help you resolve problems and feel better.

How could you apply this resilience framework to how Nazreen supported Jordan and Awais in Chapter 1?

The role of the adult: Positive relationships and enabling environments

Early years practitioners play a crucial role in helping young children build up their abilities to keep trying. This starts in the baby room. Think about the example of Ruby reaching for the toy in the last chapter. Lansbury (2012) explains very clearly the possible effects of giving Ruby the toy rather than let her persist in getting it for herself.

1. When babies are playing, it's next to impossible for us to know what they're really up to unless they show us by "doing it"... More often than not, when we offer babies the toys they seem to be looking at, we are jumping to a conclusion about their desire or intention that is false. Even if we see the infant reach toward the toy, can we be sure that the child isn't enjoying the process of stretching his arm toward the toy? Who are we to assume to know our child's plans?

2. In our children's eyes we are extremely powerful, magical, and influential. When we hand our baby a toy, we send this subtle message: "Rather than do whatever you are doing, take this. This is something that should interest you (or that I want you to be using)."

> Children often display faulty logic because, like all of us throughout life, they build their learning on what they know and understand. The skilful practitioner listens for that understanding and tunes into the child's process rather than leaping into corrective mode.

3. And the less subtle message: "Don't bother trying to move, I'll get that for you."

4. And even more crippling: "You need me to get toys for you."

So, amazingly, by the innocent act of handing a baby a toy, we send discouraging, defeating messages that can hinder development and create unnecessary dependencies. We also rob children of the invaluable opportunity to feel competent and experience mastery.

Of course we have to remember that underpinning Ruby's efforts is a loving relationship with her mother. We should not expect children to be resilient and persistent if they are not secure in knowing they are loved and cherished for who they are and supported, as well as challenged in their learning.

Children often display faulty logic because, like all of us throughout life, they build their learning on what they know and understand. The skilful practitioner listens for that understanding and tunes into the child's process rather than leaping into corrective mode.

Have a look at the example on page 34 and the diagram on page 35. We see the practitioner using the observation, assessment and planning cycle here as she assesses 'in the moment '

Pause for thought

- How does your key person system work to help you in really getting to know the children in your care?

- Do you regularly talk with parents about children's achievements in being persistent and controlling their own learning?

- Have you considered running some informal workshops for parents on how children learn?

As children get older and being to develop their language skills it is important to talk with them about their learning and to be aware of the language you are using that encourage active learning.

Assessing in the moment

A group of three and four-year-olds are engaged in discussion about making a whale to go with some other sea creatures they have talked about and made.

The conversation	What is the practitioner doing?
Practitioner: Let's look at the picture in the book … Who can remember what these are?	Encouraging recall of previous learning. Questioning. Allowing time for thinking about the answer.
Ava: I know, I know … several seconds pause (practitioner and the other children wait expectantly, practitioner puts her hand on the arm of Ethan who looks like he is going to interrupt and says 'Let Ava have time to think'.	Being explicit about the importance of thinking time.
Ava: Bar, bar, barsicles *(smiling broadly)*.	
Practitioner: Good thinking – you remembered barnacles.	Praises Ava's thinking and repeats important vocabulary ('remembered'). Feeds back the correct version of the word (recasts) rather than correcting Ava.
Ava: Oh yes barnacles they stick on the side and never do come off.	
Ethan: I saw a big giant fish it and it was called a crocodile.	Allows children time to have a learning conversation amongst them. Not all conversation is routed through her.
Ben: A crocodile isn't a fish.	
Ethan: Yes, it swims in the water.	
Ben: But it's not a fish.	
Ethan: It is, it is and it's big like a whale and it has lots of teeth.	
Practitioner: Ben what do you think a crocodile is?	
Ben *(shrugs and smiles)***:** Don't know but it's not a fish it's got legs.	
Practitioner: That's true, good thinking Ben.	Praises thinking again.
Elsa *(interrupting)***:** When are we going to make the whale, I got some things ready *(indicates scissors black material, glue, paper of various colours)*.	Allows children to determine the focus.
Ava: Yea let's do the whale.	
At this point Ben picks up some black material waves it over his head and says 'Let's rock and roll'. The others laugh.	
Practitioner: Ok let's start the whale but let's keep thinking about what sort of creatures whales and crocodiles are. We might be able to find something in a book or on the computer to help us later.	Reminds the children about the debate they are having and refers to sources of support. Does not supply the answers herself.

Observation, Assessment and Planning cycle

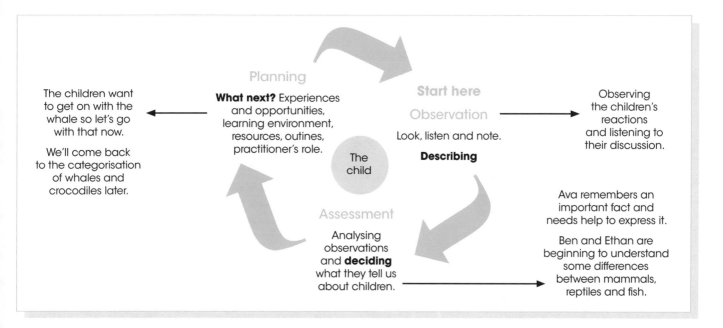

Planning

What next? Experiences and opportunities, learning environment, resources, outines, practitioner's role.

The children want to get on with the whale so let's go with that now.

We'll come back to the categorisation of whales and crocodiles later.

Start here

Observation

Look, listen and note.

Describing

The child

Observing the children's reactions and listening to their discussion.

Ava remembers an important fact and needs help to express it.

Ben and Ethan are beginning to understand some differences between mammals, reptiles and fish.

Assessment

Analysing observations and **deciding** what they tell us about children.

How do you see this cycle being used in this example? Cameron (aged four) is sitting on a coach on a trip to the airport:

Cameron: Elephants are not allowed on the motorway

Practitioner: Perhaps they would be allowed in a horsebox?

Cameron: *(Laughs and then says patiently)* No, it would be too small and it would be an elephant box, but they're not allowed anyway.

Practitioner: How do you know they're not allowed?

Cameron: There was a sign back there that said it.

Practitioner: Are you sure?

Cameron: Yes it was there *(pointing back down motorway)* I was the practitioner and at this point I was mystified but kept my eyes open for the sign Cameron had seen when we were returning later in the day. And there it was – a brown tourist sign with these two symbols and some writing:

Cameron may have been wrong about what the print actually said, but I was full of respect for his learning power. We had been doing some work on road safety and he had generalised from information and experience that a cross on a road sign means not allowed. My assessment was that he had used all the knowledge he had to persist in understanding something he had seen and which he realised contains meaning. As Bruce (2001) says: *'Learning is only partly about learning new things. It is mainly about using what is already known, in flexible and imaginative ways'.*

Children need practitioners to reflect on Bruce's point and think about how children can be encouraged to build learning power like Cameron's. Claxton (2006) says: *'Effective support can easily create dependency, and encourages us instead to 'look for a way to do less, to hand the control back to the students'.* If we keep on trying to teach children more and more new information and skills without really observing what they can do with what they already know, we will miss chances to support and extend their capabilities as learners. Questions are important in finding out more and allowing us to make accurate assessments and plan accordingly. But they need to be mainly open-ended and genuine.

'Tania would you like to close the window it's cold?' is not genuine – it's really a command thinly disguised as a question. Holding up a red object and asking 'What colour is this?' is not open-ended – there is only one right answer. Claxton suggests some more open-ended questions we could be asking ourselves and young learners:

- How did you do that?

- How else could you have done that?

- Who did that a different way?

- What was hard about doing that?

- What could you do when you are stuck on that?

- How could you help someone else do that?

- What would have made that easier for you?

- How could I have taught that better?

- How could you make that harder for yourself?

Keeping on trying not to do something – the marshmallow test

This may seem a strange idea but it's important, as anyone who has ever been on a diet, revised for an exam or saved money will know. Sometimes we need to be able to 'delay gratification' that is put off doing something right now because in the long run that is a better plan for us. Eating a lot of chocolate, going out socialising or spending a large sum of money on clothes are all things we might enjoy in the short term, but in the long term they won't help us achieve our goal to lose weight, pass the exam or buy a car.

In 1972, Professor Walter Mischel conducted some experiments with four-year-olds to try and find out if young children were capable of delaying gratification. The children were left in a room sitting at a table with a marshmallow on a plate in front of them. They were told that if they wanted to they could eat it immediately but if they waited for 15 minutes they would be able to have another one as well. About one third of the children ate the marshmallow right away, another third managed to hold out for a few minutes and the rest resisted temptation and got two marshmallows.

"What we're really measuring with the marshmallows isn't will power or self-control," Mischel says. "It's much more important than that. This task forces kids to find a way to make the situation work for them. They want the second marshmallow, but how can they get it? We can't control the world, but we can control how we think about it." Mischel discovered that the children who could wait and delay gratification had that sort of thought control. They distracted themselves by covering their eyes, pretending to play hide-and-seek underneath the table, or singing songs. The good news is that he has since discovered that when children are taught some simple strategies, like pretending the marshmallow is only a picture, even those who could previously wait less than a minute could then manage fifteen.

We will come back to praise and recognition and its role in active learning in the next chapter but first here's a story from the adult world about the benefits of keeping on trying.

In 1953, three staff at the Rocket Chemical Company set out to create a line of rust-prevention solvents and degreasers for use in the aerospace industry. It took them 40 attempts to get the water displacing formula worked out. WD-40 stands for Water Displacement achieved on the 40th try!

Pause for thought: we teach children through what we praise

Which of these do you praise children for most often?

- Trying hard and sticking at something

- Being first with an answer

- Being quick at completing a task

- Taking time and thinking hard

- Being kind and helping others to stick at something

- Solving a problem after a lot of trial and error

- Improving on previous performance by returning to a problem or challenge.

Chapter 4: Children enjoying achieving what they set out to do

In Chapter 1 we looked at the differences between intrinsic motivation that comes from within the child and motivation that is extrinsic – where the child does things, not for the enjoyment of them for their own sake, but because it will lead to the approval of others. This chapter explores the differences between these forms of motivation in more detail.

The Early Years Foundation Stage deliberately adds 'what they set out to do' to the idea of enjoying achievement in order to emphasise that it's about intrinsic motivation where **children work to achieve their own goals**, not what adults set out for them or tell them to do. The quote above from Schweinhart and Weikart, (referring to High Scope – see Chapter 3) reminds us about the dangers of going for adult directed activities and short term impact at the cost of giving children the skills that result in life long achievement – both academic and social.

If we think back to the examples of involvement in Chapter 2 we can see that where the involvement was at level 4 and 5 there were also high levels of intrinsic motivation. Ruby struggles and keeps on trying until she succeeds. Kai Lin is involved with Simon in a joint endeavour and she knows the activity is leading to a good result for her. She is not, like Jamal, doing a non-challenging activity to pass the time until she can do something more important to her; or, like Jordan, consigning an activity the adult has asked her to do to last on her list of current interests.

We looked at the experience of Ruby, Jamal, Kai-Lin and Jordan when we were thinking about the close relationship of well-being to involvement and concentration. The emotional underpinnings of learning have also been explored through examples of the importance of the adult role in providing the positive relationships and enabling environments that encourage motivation. Although this chapter is all about children following their own ideas and fascinations, it also explores how adults can support them.

What do we mean by 'enjoying'?

In this context enjoyment involves taking pleasure in learning but it is not the same, or as simple as having fun. Fun is light hearted and often involves laughter and a shared experience whereas enjoyment is something deeper as Judith Lasater says:

> 'There's a difference between fun and enjoyment. Fun is something I might want to do to get away from my life and enjoyment is something I can bring into my life. … It is the attitude I have within my life'.

Enjoyment is an emotional response and makes us feel good when we meet our goals. This is because good things are happening in our brains. When our learning connects to prior knowledge and /or positive emotional experience, the brain 'pays attention' and stores it more readily in our memories. David Whitebread gives an example of how this connection works in the case of prior knowledge.

He suggests looking at these three words for five seconds then covering them up and trying to write them down.

Constantinople   Gwrzcwydactlmp   χονοτονπνοπλξ

He says that you probably: *"found the first one relatively easy, the second one difficult and the third (unless you read Greek) completely impossible. This is clearly related to the extent to which you can connect these new pieces of information to your existing knowledge. The first is bristling with connections you already know, at several levels (meaning, phonic sounds, letters) whereas it is increasingly difficult to make any connections with the other two"* (Whitebread, 2012: 108).

That example was relatively straightforward and if you tried it, it is unlikely to have triggered strong emotion – however we all have emotional memory systems. Recent developments in psychology and neuroscience have made clear that the whole process of perceiving, thinking, interpreting and coming to understand anything is driven by emotion and writers like Daniel Goleman (1995) have heightened public interest in 'emotional intelligence'.

The intensity of any memory is often determined by its emotional pull. The standard memory question that researchers used to ask is: "Where were you and what were you doing when President Kennedy was assassinated?". People who were alive at the time tend to remember because the event was so vivid and powerful emotionally. A more up-to-date UK question might be "Where were you and what were you doing when you heard that Princess Diana had died?" And of course, as well as these sorts of collective memories, we all have our personal memories which can bring back any number of emotions – joy, grief, pain, embarrassment, for example.

It is for this reason that advertisers, preachers and politicians use stories and scenes that are intended to tug at our heartstrings and stir basic emotions – they want us to remember the products or the religious or political messages through that emotional association with them.

Equally we know that the positive emotion of enjoyment can support children to remember their learning.

What does enjoyment of learning look like in children?

Staff at Pen Green centre in Northamptonshire look for children with a sense of 'chuffedness' – the body language which shows confidence and delight in their own achievement. Often this body language involves smiles but not always. When Ruby (in Chapter 3) finally reached her toy, after a struggle involving her whole body and a lot of intense concentration, she did not smile but put it straight in her mouth to explore. Her chuffedness was seen in her relaxed posture and evident absorption in mouthing the toy. When Jago at the end of Chapter 1 gets the two silver balls together outside the box he looks pleased (chuffed), sits back to admire them and smiles briefly before getting re-engaged in putting them back in the box. Both these children are enjoying the achievement of self chosen goals. Very importantly they also have parents who notice the process they are going through and let them work towards their goals without interfering by interrupting the process and doing it for them.

Ruby and Jago are very young and demonstrate how early our ability to identify and evaluate our own progress towards goals develops. You might think they would be more likely to get absorbed in learning as they are not yet interested in playmates to the extent that rising three to five-year-olds are and are therefore less likely to be distracted. However this drive to make sense and achieve one's own goals can, if nurtured properly, continues throughout life and social relationships play a key part in learning, they are not a distraction.

Nancy Stewart draws on some of the research in the area of children's feelings of success or failure when she says:

"Two-year-olds already know their capabilities, and show different reactions to their successes and failures according to whether they believe the task was challenging or easy for them – they show more pride with success in difficult tasks, and more shame in failing to manage easy tasks" (Stewart, 2011, p.60).

So, with the right support, children are unafraid to face challenging tasks and indeed get more satisfaction and enjoyment from rising to those challenges than they do from completing easier tasks.

Goals to support intrinsic motivation

In Chapter 3, when discussing why we keep on trying, three innate psychological drives were mentioned. We are all born with these internal motivators, which Deci and Ryan (1995) have described as drives for …

- Competence – to have the ability, knowledge and understanding to function in the world (sometimes known as the 'explanatory' drive)

- Autonomy – to be in control of our own actions and decisions

Case study – being absorbed in a process

Mia and Charisse are both four. They are sitting on the floor with two baskets. One basket is full of beads in various shades of green and the other holds blue beads. Each basket holds about 50 beads. They have a large (A2) white sheet of paper between them. Mia places about 20 green beads in a circle about 25cms in diameter in the middle of the paper and says 'That's the monster's head'. Charisse puts some blue beads at the top of the paper and says 'That's the tail'. Mia looks at her in consternation and says 'But he hasn't got a body yet!' Charisse laughs and shrugs. Mia says nothing but looks puzzled and her posture is tense, her shoulders go up and she frowns.

Charisse starts placing alternate green and blue beads diagonally in a line from the tail to the head while Mia watches. At this point Charisse is very absorbed and looking happy and Mia's body language and posture is still tense 'That's the body' says Charisse. Mia looks at it with concentration and almost immediately starts adding another parallel line of alternating green and blue beads. 'It's too thin' she says by way of explanation. She is now looking happy and relaxed again.

'Let's put on legs now' says Charisse. 'How many' says Mia 'Shall we do three?' Charisse nods. The three legs are long lines of beads in random blue/green lines coming down the paper from the body. Mia adds two blue beads at right angles to the bottom of each leg. 'Are they boots?' asks Charisse. 'Feet' says Mia. 'He should look fierce let's do a big mouth with teeth like a Wild Thing' 'and eyes' says Charisse 'and hair and ears'.

Charisse fetches black wool for the hair. The beads run out and they find sticks to make the mouth. They are serious but relaxed and communicate with few words but seem in tune with each other and both issue occasional commands, like 'Wait' and 'Stay there'. Mia goes outside to fetch some small white stones from the flower bed to make the teeth. Sam and Jay come inside with Mia and stand watching them. Jay goes over to the shelves and comes back with a tray full of corks. 'You could use these' he says as he puts the tray down beside Mia who says 'Thanks' and starts putting a line of corks along the creature's back.

Charisse goes over to the shelves and comes back with a tray of plastic bottle tops. She starts framing the work by putting a long line of tops all the way round. The boys watch in silence until Sam says: 'Can I play?'. The girls ignore him. After another two minutes Sam and Jay go back outside. Mia goes outside again and comes back with a bucket full of gravel. She and Charisse sprinkle the gravel in the remaining white spaces. 'Shall we make a pen for him?' says Charisse. 'We could use blocks. You stay there in case anyone stands on him.' She goes to the block area and comes back with a toy buggy full of unit blocks she tips them carefully beside Mia and returns for another two loads. Mia builds a wall two-blocks high round the paper, carefully placing the blocks so as to avoid disturbing any of the placed material.

This whole process has taken about 20 minutes and the girls hardly seem to be aware of anyone else, even when the noise level rises as everyone comes in from outside and practitioners are talking to the other children about tidying up and there is a lot movement to and fro and the empty trays they have been using are removed. When the wall of blocks meets to their satisfaction they both stand up and look down at their creation smiling. They look at each other still smiling. Then it seems they realise that everyone else has come in from outside and several children and one of the practitioners are clustered around them talking about their work.

Mia and Charisse seem to be in the state of 'flow' described by Csikszentmihalyi (1979) that we encountered in Chapter 2 in relation to Laura's involvement and concentration in her sand play. His research shows that in the right sort of conditions, adults dealing with problems in their field of expertise also experience a sort of pleasure and bliss just like Mia and Charisse's as they go about their work so that time really does seem to stand still.

Mia and Charisse seem very proud as the result of the joint struggle to represent their monster to their mutual satisfaction. It took a lot of commitment and linking of ideas, as well as prior knowledge of where to obtain materials and they were supported by an enabling environment for learning.

- Relatedness – to experience well-being and belonging in loving relationships.

It is these drives that keep the baby focused on learning to walk and talk and in the state of 'exuberant learning' mentioned by Carol Dweck (see page 29).

What we see illustrated in the case of Mia and Charisse, opposite, is in fact that:

> "*Like other human drives, that explanatory drive comes equipped with certain emotions: a deeply disturbing dissatisfaction when you can't make sense of things and a distinctive joy when you can*" (Gopnik, 1999: 162).

Mia is uncomfortable, both physically and emotionally, when she doesn't understand how Charisse can do the tail before the body of the monster. She is having to deal with cognitive dissonance in other words she is grappling with two ideas that contradict: her own notion that there is an order to representing a body that starts with head, then body, then tail and that all are joined in sequence and Charisse's conviction that you can leave a space where the body might be and do another part first. When any of us is confronted with two seemingly contradictory ideas, both of which seem to be true, we are thrown into genuine emotional and personal turmoil until the contradiction is resolved. That resolution is usually satisfying and brings with it a strong sense

of relief which could be seen in Mia's body language when she realised that Charisse's idea worked just as well as hers.

As John Bransford (2000) reminds us, brain research shows us that as people learn about the world in meaningful ways that matter to them, the learning changes them both mentally and physically. Working with Charisse and making their joint monster really mattered to Mia so she was prepared to endure the discomfort of accepting a different way of doing things and was thus rewarded with some powerful learning.

Both children had autonomy as they were in control of what they were doing. It was their decision to represent a monster by the ways in which they placed the beads and other materials on paper. They were not told to do something about a monster but used their own interest in *Where the Wild Things Are*. They decided how to proceed with every step and felt confident to fetch resources as needed from around the nursery.

Clearly this experience was social and collaborative and answered the children's drive for relatedness. They were accepting of each other's contributions and both saw this as a joint enterprise with a joint goal.

Performance goals

'Goal Theory' is a term used in educational psychology to discuss research into motivation to learn. Generally there are two types of goal for which people aim.

- Mastery goals

- Performance goals.

Mastery goals are clearly **linked with intrinsic motivation** in that they include achieving a sense of mastery through developing new skills and understandings, becoming more competent and doing the best one can for one's own satisfaction. An example at adult level might be a practitioner who is fascinated by children's learning and wants to know more so she can become a more effective early years worker. She enrols on a course of further professional development to help her achieve that goal. She is likely to be very committed to the process of learning, as it will have impact on things that really matter to her personally – the children she works with and her own understanding of their learning and her teaching. She may be pleased if she gets good marks, but that is not the

main driver for her continuing commitment to the course and to becoming the best practitioner she can be – that goal will continue long after the course has finished.

Performance goals are directly **related to extrinsic motivation** and focus on ability and self image rather than one's own desire to learn. An adult example might be the practitioner who enrols on a course of further professional development not because of her own interest, but because her manager tells her she is under-qualified and if she wants to progress within the organisation she better get a higher level of qualification.

Performance goals like these can be great in the short term, as they may spur us on to do things we hadn't considered, but they also have some downsides. By their nature they are rather shallow and not likely to inspire commitment to the process. With this goal set by the manager, and where the practitioner does not feel the need for the qualification, it is more likely (unless the experience of going on the course changes her goal) that she will only exert herself to get good marks by concentrating solely on things that she can use in assignments or exams. She may even feel ok about cheating in an exam or assignment to get good marks.

Performance goals also tend to undermine long-term performance. If you hit your initial goal, you become less

motivated to continue towards excellence (after all you hit your goal). In this case the practitioner has the qualification; it's the piece of paper and getting the manager off her back that matters. And if she doesn't hit her initial goal, perhaps she fails or gives up the course, she will become discouraged and de-motivated because her self-worth is based on these external inputs. For her the outcome is based on her performance in relation to others and on receiving praise from others.

Mastery goals are clearly linked to the drives for competence, autonomy and relatedness and increase intrinsic motivation. Mia and Charisse were in a context where it was fine to spend as much time as they did on their project and where the practitioners and other children were interested in both the process of monster construction and the final outcome.

Think how motivation might have been diminished for Mia and Charisse if they had been told by their teacher to take the beads and paper to a corner of the room and make a monster with them. It is likely that they might not have been so willing to work together for an extended period but would have done the task as quickly as possible in order to get on to something they really wanted to do. The opportunities for being involved and concentrating, keeping on trying and making connections in their learning, for learning from each other and for feeling a sense of mastery and control would have been reduced or even lost.

Children with mastery goals are interested in learning new skills and improving their understanding and competence, whereas those with performance goals are more concerned with proving their ability or avoiding negative judgments of their competence. There is a clear link here with Carol Dweck's work on fixed and growth mindsets, already touched on in Chapters 1 and 3. Her research has identified that children develop mindsets by an early age:

> "We offered four year olds a choice: they could redo an easy jigsaw, or they could try a harder one. Even at this tender age, children with the fixed mindset – the ones that believed in fixed traits – stuck with the safe one… Children with the growth mindset – the ones who believed you could get smarter – thought it was a strange choice. 'Why are you asking me this lady? Why would anyone want to keep doing the same puzzle over and over. They chose one hard on after another" (Dweck, 2006: 16).

Extrinsic motivation – rewards and praise

Stickers and star charts

Attempting to encourage positive behaviour in children through the liberal use of stickers and star charts is based on the assumption that children are only motivated to act positively in response to a reward. It also places the practitioners in sole charge of the learning if it's only been done to get the sticker or star. Those children who find it hardest to work out what the adult wants and to comply are at risk of being publicly labelled failures through their obvious lack of stars or stickers. If everyone gets stickers regularly they lose any meaning they might have had in motivating or modifying behaviour (see Chapter 1).

A study conducted in the 1970s, for example, showed that when children got a ribbon and a gold star for drawing pictures they spent less time drawing later. Children who received no reward or only occasionally and unexpectedly got a reward, continued to be motivated to make pictures.

Another risk is that children focus entirely on performance goals and do not value their own ideas, they want stickers all the time – sometimes this can be a competition with others. Many practitioners will have worked with children who are always bringing them pictures, bits of writing or models that have been thrown together but they want adult praise all the time – almost as if they are addicted to it. Some will be very conscious that their performance oriented parents will ask them later about the number of stickers they received.

My experience is that star charts work for short periods of time with some children who have quite specific behavioural difficulties when they have a large amount of control of the chart, deciding for themselves with practitioner support and encouragement when they get a star and never ever losing stars, as happens in some places.

Praise

Carol Dweck's research indicates that fixed mindsets can be changed by paying attention to the ways in which we praise children. Most early years practitioners believe that praise is important in motivating children and recognising achievement. But we need to be careful with it. Carol Dweck claims:

> "After seven experiments with hundreds of children, we had some of the clearest findings I've ever seen. Praising children's intelligence harms their motivation and it harms their performance" (Dweck, 2006, p.175).

This may seem very surprising as we know children love praise but let's think about what and how we praise. Reflect on these examples:

- Good boy you made that so quickly, you are clever

- You're so brilliant, I am so proud of you coming first in the race

- Good girl, I love your picture.

You might consider these to be supportive messages but think again about the hidden message the child may be hearing.

Examples of praise

Practitioner says	Child hears
Good boy you made that so quickly, you are clever	If I don't make something quickly, I'm not good and I'm not clever
You're so brilliant, I am so proud of you coming first in the race	If I don't come first I'm not brilliant
Good girl, I love your picture	I am a good person when you love what I do

So with this sort of praise the child gets a special glow but it will not last. As soon as they hit a difficulty, their confidence, which is based on other people's approval, goes out the window and their motivation decreases. If success means they are good and clever and please you, failure means they are bad, stupid and don't please you – not a good basis on which to continue making the effort to learn. If practitioners establish caring warm relationships with young children, those children will want practitioners' approval and will be very interested in their reactions to everything they do.

It Is a great pity if well-meaning adults undermine children's confidence by neglecting to praise children for effort rather than intelligence or natural ability. When we do this, children feel different and motivation remains high.

Consider these alternatives:

Examples of praise

Practitioner says	Child hears
Wow you worked really hard to make that, well done	My effort is noticed and praised
You really put your heart and soul into your running, how did it feel?	Running as fast as I could was hard work but it made me feel great – I can evaluate my own efforts and the process I went through
You really thought about the colours you used which part of the picture do you like best?	My thought process is valued and I can evaluate the finished result

All three alternatives praise effort and help the child feel in charge and autonomous, as well as giving them your approval. The message is clear that **you value their effort and that they can evaluate their own learning**.

Let's think back to the scenario in Chapter 1 where Abi and Connor are building a tower and their learning is scaffolded and supported by Leroy who is a more experienced builder. (See page 10) Nazreen, the practitioner does not appear to have a large role in supporting active learning. However her role in taking a photo and 'complimenting them on their joint achievement' is crucial. Let's look at what she said.

Nazreen: "This is a very tall tower and I saw how well you all worked together to make it so tall. Is it wobbly?". Abi (points at Leroy) and says: "No, he did help us". Connor smiles and says: "It won't never fall down now". Nazreen says: "Leroy, that was kind of you to help Connor and Abi." Then, smiling at Abi and Connor "I wonder if there is something you would like to say to Leroy?" They both say "Thank you". Leroy beams. Nazreen is called by another practitioner and walks away.

Notice that:

- Nazreen does not say "Good girl", "Good boy", "you're really clever".

- She focuses on the process of working together. She does not focus on correcting grammar (although she notices it).

- Nazreen smiles and looks happy.

- She encourages the children to remember about saying thank you but does not order them to do so.

- The children know why she is pleased.

- The fact that they repeat the process shows their motivation and involvement and this motivation is supported by Nazreen's words and actions.

Pause for thought

- Think about the words you use when you praise children. What sort of mindset are you encouraging? Look at these 'Forty One Ways to Say Well Done' (N. Stewart) – can you add to them?

  ○ You remembered!

  ○ You're working really hard.

  ○ One more time and you'll have it.

  ○ You chose a hard way – you'll learn from that!

  ○ It looks like you've been practising!

  ○ (Child's name) looked really happy when you did that.

  ○ I've never seen one like that before.

  ○ That was a kind thing to do.

  ○ Look at you go!

  ○ Keep it up.

  ○ You've figured that out yourself.

  ○ I can see you …(describe details of what child has done).

  ○ Good remembering.

  ○ I like the way you…

  ○ That is interesting.

  ○ You're on the right track now.

  ○ Keep working on it, you're nearly there.

  ○ You are learning fast.

  ○ You tried a few different ways.

  ○ Good for you!

  ○ That's the way.

  ○ You've got the hang of that.

  ○ You're looking really carefully.

  ○ I think you've got it now.

  ○ You're trying to do even more!

  ○ You're learning a lot about that.

  ○ That's an interesting idea.

  ○ You've been concentrating on that.

  ○ Good going! You kept trying.

  ○ You've found a new way to do it.

  ○ You've done it just like you said you would.

  ○ I think you've got it now.

  ○ Good thinking. That does make sense.

  ○ You haven't missed a thing.

  ○ You tried harder and harder.

  ○ You knew just what to do.

  ○ I bet you're pleased with that.

  ○ You really paid attention.

  ○ You worked so carefully.

  ○ That's it! It works!

  ○ Which do you think is the best part?

Stewart (2012) used with kind permission

Tuning-in to what children are doing is sometimes difficult in a busy setting and requires one to act like children do when they join in – watching and looking from the sidelines in preparation. In the following example the practitioner has shown positive interest but has not really tuned in.

Jack, Kayleigh, Kyle and Imran are playing in wet sand. They have been speaking very little but their play involves a lot of stirring up the sand with sticks. Jack says a couple of times 'It will explode soon' and Kayleigh and Imran mention the 'Omnitrix'. A practitioner approaches from the far side of room.

Practitioner: What are you doing?

Jack: Just making a mixture.

Practitioner: What's in your mixture?

Kayleigh: Scrambled eggs and pie.

Practitioner: Can I have some?

Kayleigh: It's not ready yet.

Kyle and Imran have remained silent and look down during this exchange. When the practitioner leaves the area the children look at each other and laugh. They then continue with the play. About two minutes later Jack begins a count down ' 5, 4, 3, 2, 1,' all four children shout 'Blast Off' together and throw a handful of sand each into the air. They run off to continue the play elsewhere.

The children are very happy playing with each other and sharing their joint interest in Ben 10®. They appear on other

- The photos Nazreen takes will be used later to help all three children recall their learning – a crucial part of the process of learning to think about one's own thinking and a vital stage in becoming a self regulated learner.

And of course, we must remember that children need unconditional recognition for themselves, not just for their learning. "I am really pleased to see you today Charlie. We missed you yesterday" helps a child feel valued for himself – without that sense of well-being and connection the confidence to take on the challenges of learning will not be supported and nurtured.

The role of the adult: positive relationships and enabling environments

We saw how the social relationship between Mia and Charisse helped them sustain their interest and involvement in the monster making activity. Peer relationships help children in their drive for relatedness – the sense of well-being and belonging mentioned earlier. Adults are important too and belonging to a community can support motivation. It is adults who can really make the group, the class, the whole setting or school, a **learning community**. This requires adults to focus on groups as well as individuals, to listen carefully and to join in sensitively with the play.

Pause for thought

- How often do children in your setting get to play with or alongside children who are younger or older then themselves and how big are the potential age ranges?

- George and Leila's nursery in the example below is organised in family groups so all key groups are mixed age. What do you think might be the opportunities and challenges offered by this way of grouping children?

occasions to be very happy and relaxed sharing ideas with the practitioner but they have obviously decided that Ben 10® is either not her interest or it's something they want to keep to themselves at the moment.

A sense of community is built when children learn together and from each other. Children learn about their own competence and get involved in activities through watching and imitating other children. Kayleigh was the oldest child in that group and the others deferred to her invention of the scrambled eggs and pie – another example of how children learn many things we may not plan!

George is 11-months-old. He is participating in a heuristic play session with another 11-month-old baby, an 18-month-old toddler and Leila, a three-year-old who has asked if she can join the babies.

George puts his arms through the cardboard cylinders babbling and smiling to himself. Occasionally he looks at his key person for reassurance.

He picks up a cone-shaped shell from the floor and carefully inserts it into one of the cylinders and takes it out several times.

Then he watches Leila who is putting small round pieces of foam from a tin into paper cups. He watches and babbles then picks up a wooden curtain ring and holds it out to Leila. She ignores him at first, but when he babbles more loudly and continues to hold out the ring she takes it and puts it in a cup. He picks up the cup and squashes it in his hands with the ring still inside it, before putting it in his mouth.

Leila picks up all the remaining cups and stacks them inside each other. Then she takes the top one, puts a curtain ring in it and places it in front of George (who is still happily mouthing the first cup and ring) Then Leila turns her body away from him placing the cups nearer to herself and further from him.

Here we see George motivated by both the heuristic play and his interest in Leila. Leila is clear that she does not really want to play with him but is also prepared to think about his wants whilst, at the same time, organising the resources so that she can continue undisturbed with the interest she has. She has already shown her understanding of how the baby room is organised for heuristic play. When she entered the room she started talking but when one of the practitioners put her finger to her lips and indicated what was happening she imitated her sign and sat down silently. The same practitioner has been

> A sense of community is built when children learn together and from each other. Children learn about their own competence and get involved in activities through watching and imitating other children.

watching the interaction between George and Leila but has not stepped in to help as she sees them managing ok on their own.

Building a learning community involves being very tuned-in to the children's own learning power and nurturing and extending children's motivation to learn. Practitioners can ensure that the positive relationships they build with children aim to…

- Talk about learning, rather than just directing

- Support children by describing what they see them trying to do

- Stimulate children's interest through shared attention.

Talking about learning

A true learning conversation involves using the words, attitudes and actions of a learner. Even with babies and toddlers saying things like 'You remembered, it's socks next' rather than 'pass me the socks' emphasises the child's responsibility for their own learning. This lays the foundations for getting older children involved in setting their own goals, making plans, and reviewing their own progress and successes. As Lilian Katz says:

> "*If teachers want their young pupils to have robust dispositions to investigate, hypothesize, experiment, conjecture and so forth, they might consider making their own such intellectual dispositions more visible to the children*" (Katz, 1995, p.65).

She goes on to regret the lack of conversations that start with practitioners saying things like "I've been wondering if this the best time to…" or "I'm not sure if this is the best place to put this. Anybody got any ideas?" or "when I thought about your question I thought the answer might be…it would be interesting to find out what the answer is". When we talk like this we model our enthusiasm for thinking and we show how it can be a struggle – but one that is deeply satisfying and involving. We show we are 'in love with ideas' as Marion Dowling suggests (see page 25) and we supply the vocabulary for manipulating those ideas and getting involved in thinking.

Supporting children by describing what you see them trying to do

The development of language is crucial for thinking. Many children come to settings from homes where they have heard lots of words and that makes a difference to their vocabulary. We also know that vocabulary at the age of two is a good indicator of future success – the more words you know and use, the more likely you are do better in later life.

Practitioners therefore play a key role in helping children, particularly those who have not had a rich language environment at home, to understand and use words. This may be as simple as…

- When baby similes and babble at sight of food repeating 'dinner' several times.

- With a toddler: "You are putting the pasta in the cup, now you're pouring it out, in the cup out of the cup".

> **Children have lots of interests but sometimes they need us to stimulate and support an interest that may not be immediately appealing.**

- With a three-year-old: "You are making a line with the cars, will they fit on the carpet?".

- With a four or five-year-old: "You are leaning the pipe against the wall. I wonder if it needs some support?".

Notice that these comments show you are interested in the child's activity and any questions are related to what the practitioner observes is the child's concern. They also encourage children to talk about their own processes and successes. Again this links with valuing effort over immediate results and focuses on paying attention to what the child is doing.

Stimulating children's interest through shared attention

In the examples above we see joint attention in action – the practitioner and the child are both paying attention to the same process. Children have lots of interests but sometimes they need us to stimulate and support an interest that may not be immediately appealing. Nancy Stewart quotes Bandura (1994):

> "*Most of the things people enjoy doing for their own sake originally held little or no interest for them. Children are not born innately interested in singing operatic arias, playing contrabassoons, solving mathematical equations or propelling shot-put balls through the air*" (Stewart, 2011, p.65).

Clearly it is not our business in early years to start teaching opera singing or any of these other advanced skills to young children. However it is our attention to music that may spark the eventual interest in singing. We help children to take the first step along the way.

If we think that children may need help to access the many forms of music and song in the world do we draw their attention to some of it? Is music more than a background noise and do we make and listen to it together, trying out our voices, beginning to understand pitch and rhythm, making those first steps towards a life long interest perhaps? Do we draw children's attention to the way in which numbers work in terms of pattern and balance and the ways in which we can get better at throwing by thinking about aim, trajectory and what we do with our arm and whole body? As Stewart says:

> '*Adults have a role in supporting children to break down complex skills into sub-goals where they can experience self-*

efficacy, leading to steadily growing personal involvement and interest' (Stewart, 2011, p.65).

Building confidence to explore and take risks

Children will look to practitioners to support their explorations of the world. They are tuned-in to our attitudes to opportunities and threats in the environment. Older babies and toddlers are good at 'checking in' with their parent or caregiver to see whether what they are about to do is ok. This is known as 'social referencing'.

A well-known experiment done with babies in this area is the 'visual cliff'. A crawling baby is confronted by what looks like a drop (it is actually a plexiglass surface which is completely safe to crawl over). The mother is on the other side of the drop with a toy. All the babies involved stopped at the visual edge and looked at their mothers for a clue as to what to do. When mothers made a fear face the baby stayed put. When the mother smiled encouragingly the baby crawled across the space.

The message for practitioners is that children can be encouraged to go further to take risks if we reassure them. Think how important this is for those children who come to your setting already showing signs of a fixed mindset. Of course we have to keep children safe, but think about these questions:

- Have any of you or your colleagues communicated a dislike of spiders, worms or other creepy crawlies to the children?

- Have any children been put off rough and tumble play by practitioners thinking that if children start 'bundling' it will lead to fighting?

If we put artificial boundaries in place, children learn to be helpless. If we don't fall and get minor bumps and scrapes once in a while we will never know how much it hurts but also how quickly our body recovers. If we are not allowed to be fascinated by all living creatures, we cut ourselves off from much awe and wonder.

This chapter has begun to explore the idea of a learning community where it is the norm to work together and be involved in joint interests and endeavours because they help us remain motivated active learners. The next and final chapter

looks in more detail at leading a learning community that encourages everyone involved to be lifelong learners.

All three strands of active learning – being involved and concentrating, keeping on trying and enjoying achieving what they set out to do – contribute to children becoming better at regulating their own learning.

To really support and extend children's skills as active learners, all staff have to be committed to and understand the characteristics of effective early learning; seeing for instance how children engage with learning through and in their play and bring their creative and critical thinking skills to bear on solving problems and choosing ways to do things.

Chapter 5: Leading a thoughtful approach

"*Alison offers an open invitation to her children: it is an invitation to all comers, an invitation that she hopes they will find irresistible. It is to join her in the adventure of learning of all kinds, an opportunity for the children to extend themselves as far as and further than they may sometimes have thought possible and to do so in an environment of encouragement and interest*"

(*Hart et al., 2004, p.78*).

Leadership and management

The quote opposite comes from a book entitled *Learning without Limits*. In this final chapter we explore how we might seek to reduce limits on children's learning and reflect on how leaders and managers might offer an invitation like Alison's to children, parents and colleagues.

Some of what follows draws on the approach set out in Moylett and Stewart (2012). Leadership is often used as one half of the phrase 'leadership and management'. These are terms that are used together and often interchangeably. Most writers see them as complementary, with leadership viewed as the vision and influence to inspire and initiate change, and management being more about everyday organisation.

- In the context of **national frameworks** such as the EYFS in England, the Foundation Stage in Wales or the Curriculum for Excellence in Scotland, leaders and managers are understood to be the named person in overall charge of the setting or school.

- **Childminders** may not think of themselves as leaders and managers when working in their own homes, but they too are the person in charge, to whom children and parents turn. If they are working with colleagues or are network coordinators their role also involves leading and managing adults.

Leadership and management at any level are about learning and development. Settings, and the adults working in them, grow and develop in response to positive relationships and enabling environments – just like the children. It is the responsibility of leaders and managers to provide an ethos where this growth, development and continuous improvement can take place.

In this chapter we are going to concentrate particularly on the leadership role of the person in charge (and other senior staff in a large setting) rather than on day-to-day management. However leadership skills are not confined to the person who has ultimate responsibility for leadership in an official capacity. Children and their parents look to all early years practitioners for leadership and management as they go about the daily business of organising their group or class, making decisions and 'being in charge'. All practitioners are leaders of learning; so all readers should find some provocation for thinking here.

A thoughtful approach

A thoughtful approach is one based on reflection and the leader's concern for all the people in the community of the setting. The community of the setting includes:

- Children

- Parents

- Staff

- Other professionals and the local community.

Pause for thought

- How might you involve parents in helping their children become lifelong learners?

Everything that this book has so far discussed about working with children has been based on respecting and valuing children as powerful learners with unique personalities and attributes, who deserve to be valued for who they are, regardless of culture and background.

A setting which truly values children and families will be very likely also to value its staff.

Valuing leads to trusting and is based on staff experiencing a sense of their own value within an organisation and feeling comfortable about their own abilities and needs. Through supportive relationships within the organisation they reflect upon practice in dialogue with colleagues, and work together to create change and improvement in the setting, confident of support.

Throughout this book we have considered examples of practitioners supporting and extending children's learning. All the practitioners we have considered in action have done and said things based on their knowledge and understanding about children's entitlements to positive relationships, time, space and experiences. Underpinning all this understanding are their values and beliefs as well as the shared ethos (the way the setting feels and how people do things).

The model on page 52 represents how this cycle of professional development works in settings, not only to value all who learn and work there, but also to create a learning community for children, staff and parents.

The basis is an approach that sees practitioners, parents and children as co-researchers in children's learning. The ethos and values are those held by each individual, as well as discussed and developed together as a setting. They are informed by the principles and commitments of the EYFS or other frameworks used, as well as experience, knowledge and understanding of children's entitlements for learning and development.

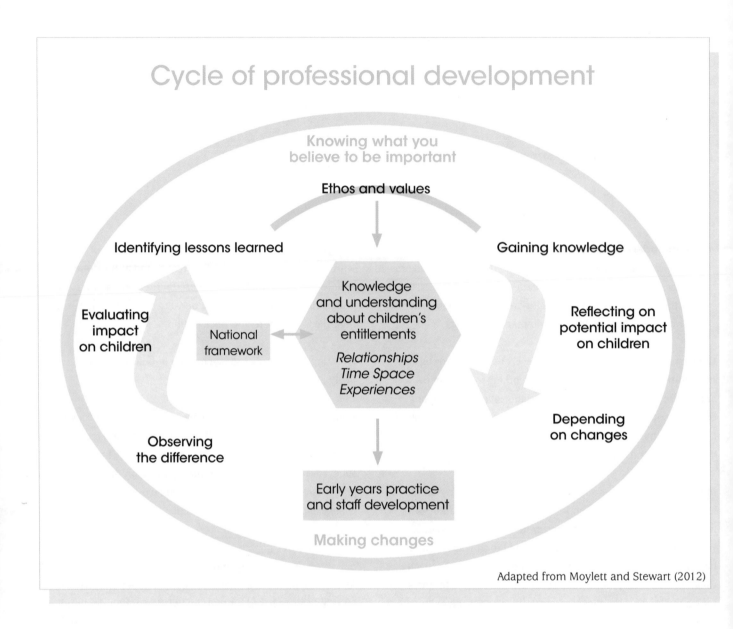

Cycle of professional development

Knowing what you believe to be important

Ethos and values

Identifying lessons learned

Gaining knowledge

Evaluating impact on children

National framework

Knowledge and understanding about children's entitlements

Relationships Time Space Experiences

Reflecting on potential impact on children

Observing the difference

Depending on changes

Early years practice and staff development

Making changes

Adapted from Moylett and Stewart (2012)

Establishing a shared ethos

How will a new member of staff or a new parent know what your setting's approach to learning is?

- By seeing it in action?

- By hearing you talk about it?

- By reading your policy document?

If you are not a childminder working on your own and don't have a written policy that all the staff (and possibly parents) have discussed and agreed, how do you know that staff and parents are all aware of some of the important issues discussed in this book about how we can best support children's learning?

A good leader ensures that the ethos is positive, that there is a shared 'vision' which means that everyone is working towards the same aims, everyone knows how they would like the children to learn and what they would like the children in to achieve, and they all work together in a consistent way to achieve these aims.

An effective leader:

- **Is reflective**. She takes time to think about how the setting works. Just as a key person gets to know the whole child, the leader gets to know the whole setting, including the parents and wider community, and uses that knowledge to assess next steps and plan for change.

- **Has excellent knowledge** of child development and early years care and education. Without that she cannot understand the processes through which children learn and the contexts which help them maximise that learning.

- **Is a team player**. She sees herself as part of the team as well as the leader. She knows that hers are not the only, or necessarily the best, ideas and values everyone's role. Staff, parents and children feel that their contributions are valued.

- **Learns from others**. She is not afraid to say she doesn't know all the answers and to learn from colleagues, parents and the children themselves in order to better support and extend everyone's learning.

- **Models good practice**. She is confident to 'lead by example' and influence the practice and thinking of staff.

- **Monitors and guides** the progress of projects, staff, inclusive practice, different ways of working, etc. This ensures that standards are high in all areas and, if difficulties arise or standards drop, she investigates the reasons with the team.

- **Organises resources effectively**. This will include elements such as staff development, equipment and time and enables staff to have what they need to implement the shared vision.

- **Is a decision maker** and supports staff to implement changes. If decisions are taken, she makes sure that all staff understand the reasons.

- **Listens and communicates** with staff, parents and children continuously and clearly – using the language of learning.

Pause for thought

The words and the language we use give powerful messages…

- 'learning', not 'work' language

- 'effort', not 'ability' language

- 'could be', not 'is' language.

Guy Claxton

That is not an exhaustive list but it covers most of the attributes a leader will need to create a learning community with an ethos that values everybody. Where do you think your strengths and areas for development lie?

As previously mentioned, this book is one of a series of three, which cover the characteristics of effective early learning.

- Playing and exploring

- **Active learning**

- Creating and thinking critically.

A leader who is interested in how children learn should understand the links between all three characteristics. We can think about the characteristics as where we get the engagement, motivation and thinking skills to be good learners and they are all underpinned by well-being. Children's early attachment relationships and their continuing feelings of

Links between the three characteristics

Social and Emotional Development Well-being	Playing and exploring Engagement	Ready
	Active Learning Motivation	Willing
	Creating and thinking critically Thinking	Able

Pause for thought

How might concentrating on helping all children to be lifelong learners help you to be more inclusive of children with special educational needs and disabilities?

Chapter 1 started by mentioning an active learner of nine months or ninety years and this is where the challenge may be. The characteristics are life-long learning skills and have no ages or stages attached to them. A baby can concentrate as well as a nine year old or a ninety year old. This may present challenges for us but we have to rise to them for the reasons John Holt declared many years ago.

"Since we cannot know what knowledge will be most needed in the future, it is senseless to try to teach it in advance. Instead, we should try to turn out people who love learning so much and learn so well that they will be able to learn whatever needs to be learned" (Holt, 1964).

More recently learning to learn has been identified as crucial for personal success and participation as citizens in an inclusive society (Education Council of the European Union 2006) and many projects all over the world are focusing on the learner as a whole person.

And, despite all this ongoing interest and activity, we just don't seem to get it in many parts of the education system. We have too many children whose capacities to be citizens of the twenty first century are being wasted like Emily's – a 15-year-old GCSE student quoted by Guy Claxton.

"I guess I could call myself smart. I mean I can usually get good grades. Sometimes I worry though that I'm not equipped

emotional safety in the setting supported by their key person enable them to play and explore, get involved and reflect on their learning – to be ready, willing and able learners.

Chapter 1 finished with a case study (Jago exploring the balls). The same case study also concludes Chapter 1 in *Playing and exploring* and *Creating and thinking critically*. Now as we come to the end of this book we are going to look at another shared case study this time at the other end of the birth-to-five age range – reception class children exploring dragons. Like the study of Jago this emphasises the overlapping nature of the characteristics and readers of all three books will see that many of the same issues appear across the books. Jago did not separate his play from his active learning and thinking and nor do the children exploring dragons in reception (see pages 56-60).

Challenges in observation

Most practitioners are familiar with the observation, assessment and planning cycle we saw in action on page 35. It is the engine that drives most good assessment practice and helps practitioners make judgements as to children's progress. However assessing how well children are learning to learn may be unfamiliar and seem more difficult than assessing their skills and knowledge. Most practitioners are used to making judgments in relation to age or stage expectations.

'Development Matters' provides the following guidance, opposite, on what you might be observing in a child demonstrating the characteristics of effective learning. As a leader it might be useful to think about how often you see these characteristics in action in your setting.

What to observe

	A unique child: observing how a child is learning
Playing and exploring *Engagement*	**Finding out and exploring** ● Showing curiosity about objects, events and people ● Using senses to explore the world around them ● Engaging in open-ended activity ● Showing particular interests.
	Playing with what they know ● Pretending objects are things from their experience ● Representing their experiences in play ● Taking on a role in their play ● Acting out experiences with other people.
	Being willing to 'have a go' ● Initiating activities ● Seeking challenge ● Showing a 'can do' attitude ● Taking a risk, engaging in new experiences, and learning from failures.
Active learning *Willing*	**Being involved and concentrating** ● Maintaining focus on their activity for a period of time ● Showing high levels of energy, fascination ● Not easily distracted. ● Paying attention to details
	Keeping on trying ● Persisting with activity when challenges occur ● Showing a belief that more effort or a different approach will pay off ● Bouncing back after difficulties.
	Enjoying achieving what they set out to do ● Showing satisfaction in meeting their own goals ● Being proud of how they accomplished something – not just the end result ● Enjoying meeting challenges for their own sake rather than external rewards or praise.
Creating and thinking critically *Thinking*	**Having their own ideas** ● Thinking of ideas ● Finding ways to solve problems ● Finding new ways to do things
	Making links ● Making links and noticing patterns in their experience ● Making predictions ● Testing their ideas ● Developing ideas of grouping, sequences, cause and effect.
	Choosing ways to do things ● Planning, making decisions about how to approach a task, solve a problem and reach a goal ● Checking how well their activities are going ● Changing strategy as needed ● Reviewing how well the approach worked.

CASE STUDY – starting points

The interest developed with a question (something to think about): the interest developed with a question: 'Did dragons exist?'. The provocation was given to the children (aged 5+) by their teachers as part of their creative curriculum, aiming to get children to talk together, think creatively, hypothesise and problem solve. What could be the possible answers to this question?

The play developed as the children became more interested in castles, knights and dragons. It included making imaginative stories using the small world castle and figures and building castles and lots of talk - 'raise the draw bridge' using the wooden blocks. The children took on the parts of the characters they had created and gave directions and orders, "Pull up the drawbridge there's a dragon coming". They played collaboratively, concentrating for long periods of time and becoming very involved in the stories.

The teachers recorded what the children did and said using photographs and making notes and used this to plan the next steps.

The teachers invited Sir Percival the Knight and his dragon to visit the class (the knight was a member of staff) to provoke more thinking and develop the children's ideas about knights, castles and dragons. They told the story of the knight and his dragon and spoke with the children.

The conversation between them and the children developed with the children asking lots of questions. This led to even more ideas, inspiring the children, who in the following days became engaged in role play, building a castle and finding clothes to wear as well as preparing a banquet.

"The children's ideas were supported by the teachers giving them the time, space and opportunities to construct their thinking and follow their interest."

The role play grew after the knight and dragon's visit – with children creating their own stories and becoming knights, princesses, kings and queens. They made the props they needed like the castle, swords, horses, banquet food and brought in dressing up outfits from home. The children re-created things from the stories they had heard, the discussions they had with each other and the teachers and the significant moments that had been planned. The children's ideas were supported by the teachers giving them the time, space and opportunities to construct their thinking and follow their interest. Planning was based on observing the children as they were playing and involved in conversations.

Some 'real' dragons came to school along with snakes and spiders and the children began to look more closely at other types of dragons. They found out about the lives, habits and make up of bearded dragons. They were able to touch them, hold them and take a very close look which led to much discussion both at the time and afterwards. In the following days and weeks they re-created the experience through their drawing, painting, collage, clay, dough and writing.

CASE STUDY – finding the dragon's egg

One morning the children found a dragon egg underneath a cushion where it was warm. The dragon egg was 'planted' to provoke the children's responses and language as well as getting them to think about how it got there. 'What do we do next? How do we look after the egg?'. It stirred their imagination and furthered discussion.

Looking after the dragon egg progresses over several days, after it had hatched the children decided that they needed to care for it by wrapping it in a blanket, reading stories and involving him in their play.

The adults supported all of their ideas and gave them the responsibility of what to do, when and how. *The children shared their thoughts about the dragons care in a collaborative partnership, which included negotiation, planning and thinking ahead – they took this role very seriously.*

The original question that had been posed by the teachers was: 'Did dragons exist?'. They offered the question to the children as a starting point for creative thinking, active learning and play and exploration and then supported the children's growing ideas and interest by following their lead and adding in memorable, planned moments

to extend their thinking and learning. The whole experience was co-constructed in partnership between the children and the teachers with a balance of child-initiated ideas and adult led/ focused activities resulting in some deep and meaningful thinking and learning. The children were inspired to write about their experiences.

> They were finding thinking and learning irresistible, which is what we would want all children to feel at every stage of their school experience.

I wish:...

I was a dr
agn and
blo fir ant
fly

ALex

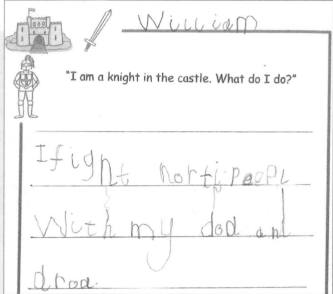

William

"I am a knight in the castle. What do I do?"

Ifignt nortj peopl
with my dad and
droa.

The children, boys and girls, were keen to write and saw this as a natural extension of their quest to find out if dragons existed.

The teachers has made sure that the writing tasks were embedded into realistic activities like invitations to the banquet, wishes and mystical stories as well as job descriptions of what a knight, princess, king, queen or dragon should do.

Writing happened anywhere and at any time.

Observing active learning

If we look at this learning story of the children's involvement in finding out if dragons existed, what can we see in relation to their active learning? The bullet points at the top of these boxes are from 'Development Matters' and are prompts for what we might observe a child doing. Underneath are some examples of what can be seen in the learning story – you might want to add more.

Being involved and concentrating	Keeping on trying	Enjoying achieving what they set out to do
• Maintaining focus on their activity for a period of time • Showing high levels of energy, fascination • Not easily distracted • Paying attention to details. Children stayed involved as the play evolved over a long period. They showed high levels of involvement in story making and took on the parts of characters they created. They were very interested in the myth or reality question. In looking after the dragon's egg they were paying a lot of attention to the details of care	• Persisting with activity when challenges occur • Showing a belief that more effort or a different approach will pay off • Bouncing back after difficulties. Children faced challenges building the castle but persisted and used various forms of support including each other and practitioners. They made props, tried various ways and found solutions, including bringing in things from home. They had to work out how to care for the egg and needed to use different skills at different times	• Showing satisfaction in meeting their own goals • Being proud of how they accomplished something – not just the end result • Enjoying meeting challenges for their own sake rather than external rewards or praise. The children developed their own goals from their ongoing experiences. Staff were there in the background, but had not planned the whole thing in advance. The children had choices and responsibility. Their intrinsic motivation kept the process going not external goals. They were proud of the whole process.

to achieve what I want, that I'm just a tape recorder repeating back what I've heard. I worry that once I'm out of school and people don't keep handing me information with questions…I'll be lost" (Claxton, 2004, p.1).

As Claxton puts it: "Emily sees herself as ready for a life of tests, but not the tests of life."

This is a sad indictment of our system. You may think we do things differently and better in early years where we do not formally test children but we can still take a long hard look at whether our observational assessments and planning really focus on the characteristics or whether we go for the easier countable things.

Whether you are a setting leader or a practitioner once you have focused on observing the characteristics in action, you may think of improvements that could be made to practice or provision. Some suggestions are provided in the Positive Relationships and Enabling Environments columns in 'Development Matters'. They were turned into an audit of the adult role in *Understanding the Revised Early Years Foundation Stage* (see next page).

However long we have been working with young children there is always more to learn and children can teach us where to take them if we tune-in to their interests. As Vivian Gussin Paley says:

"*It is in the development of their themes and characters and plots that children explain their thinking and enable us to wonder who we might become as their teachers.*"(Gussin Paley, 2004: 8)

With effective leadership, early years settings can be learning communities where learning to learn is the most important priority for staff, children and parents. If all the staff understand why the characteristics are important and regularly discuss and debate ways to improve the quality of what is offered to children both amongst themselves and with parents, the children will fly. Learning how to learn frees children from the constraints imposed by notions of 'ability'.

Development Matters: Supporting the Characteristics of Effective Learning – the adult role

	Positive Relationships: what adults could do	+ / −	Enabling Environments: what adults could provide	+ / −	What could be further developed in our practice?
Playing and exploring (engagement)					
Finding out and exploring	Play with children. Encourage them to explore, and show your own interest in discovering new things.		Provide stimulating resources which are accessible and open-ended so they can be used, moved and combined in a variety of ways.		
Playing with what they know	Help children as needed to do what they are trying to do, without taking over or directing.		Make sure resources are relevant to children's interests.		
Being willing to 'have a go'	Join in play sensitively, fitting in with children's ideas.		Arrange flexible indoor and outdoor space and resources where children can explore, build, move and role play.		
	Model pretending an object is something else, and help develop roles and stories. Be sure to support children's confidence with words and body language.		Help children concentrate by limiting noise, and making spaces visually calm and orderly.		
	Encourage children to try new activities and to judge risks for themselves.		Plan first-hand experiences and challenges appropriate to the development of the children.		
	Pay attention to how children engage in activities – the challenges faced, the effort, thought, learning and enjoyment. Talk more about the process than products.		Ensure children have uninterrupted time to play and explore.		
	Talk about how you and the children get better at things through effort and practice, and what we all can learn when things go wrong.				
Active learning (motivation)	Support children to choose their activities – what they want to do and how they will do it.		Children will become more deeply involved when you provide something that is new and unusual for them to explore, especially when it is linked to their interests.		
Being involved and concentrating	Stimulate children's interest through shared attention, and calm over-stimulated children.		Notice what arouses children's curiosity, looking for signs of deep involvement to identify learning that is intrinsically motivated.		
Keeping on trying	Help children to become aware of their own goals, make plans, and to review their own progress and successes.		Ensure children have time and freedom to become deeply involved in activities.		
Enjoying achieving what they set out to do	Describe what you see them trying to do, and encourage children to talk about their own processes and successes.		Children can maintain focus on things that interest them over a period of time. Help them to keep ideas in mind by talking over photographs of their previous activities.		
	Be specific when you praise, especially noting effort such as how the child concentrates, tries different approaches, persists, solves problems, and has new ideas.		Keep significant activities out instead of routinely tidying them away.		
	Encourage children to learn together and from each other.		Make space and time for all children to contribute.		
	Children develop their own motivations when you give reasons and talk about learning, rather than just directing.				
Creating and thinking critically (thinking)	Use the language of thinking and learning: think, know, remember, forget, idea, makes sense, plan, learn, find out, confused, figure out, trying to do.		In planning activities, ask yourself: Is this an opportunity for children to find their own ways to represent and develop their own ideas? Avoid children just reproducing someone else's ideas.		
Having their own ideas	Model being a thinker, showing that you don't always know, are curious and sometimes puzzled, and can think and find out.		Build in opportunities for children to play with materials before using them in planned tasks.		
Making links	Encourage open-ended thinking by not settling on the first ideas: What else is possible?		Play is a key opportunity for children to think creatively and flexibly, solve problems and link ideas. Establish the enabling conditions for rich play: space, time, flexible resources, choice, control, warm and supportive relationships.		
Choosing ways to do things	Always respect children's efforts and ideas, so they feel safe to take a risk with a new idea.		Recognisable and predictable routines help children to predict and make connections in their experiences.		
	Talking aloud helps children to think and control what they do.		Routines can be flexible, while still basically orderly.		
	Model self-talk, describing your actions in play.		Plan linked experiences that follow the ideas children are really thinking about.		
	Give children time to talk and think.		Use mind-maps to represent thinking together.		
	Value questions, talk, and many possible responses, without rushing toward answers too quickly.		Develop a learning community which focuses on **how** and not just what we are learning.		
	Support children's interests over time, reminding them of previous approaches and encouraging them to make connections between their experiences.				
	Model the creative process, showing your thinking about some of the many possible ways forward.				
	Sustained shared thinking helps children to explore ideas and make links. Follow children's lead in conversation, and think about things together.				
	Encourage children to describe problems they encounter, and to suggest ways to solve the problem.				
	Show and talk about strategies – how to do things – including problem-solving, thinking and learning.				
	Give feedback and help children to review their own progress and learning. Talk with children about what they are doing, how they plan to do it, what worked well and what they would change next time.				
	Model the plan-do-review process yourself.				

References

Chapter 1

Bandura, A. (1997). *Self-efficacy: The exercise of control*, Freeman, New York.

Bandura, A.(1977) *Social Learning Theory*, Englewood Cliffs, Prentice Hall, NJ.

Bronson, M. (2000) *Self-regulation in Early Childhood:Nature and Nurture*, The Guilford Press, New York.

DCSF (2008) The Early Years Foundation Stage (available only as download from www.foundationyears.org).

DCSF (2009) 'Learning, Playing and Interacting', Crown copyright (available for download at www.foundationyears.org.uk).

Dweck, C (2006) Mindset, *The New Psychology of Success*, Ballantine Books, New York.

Ministry of Education (1996) Te Whariki, Wellington: New Zealand.

Montessori Education (http://www.montessori.org.uk).

National Strategies, DCSF (2009) Learning, Playing and Interacting, Crown copyright (downloadable from www.foundationyears.org.uk).

Nolte, D.L. and Harris, R. (1998) *Children Learn What They Live*, New York (Workman Publishing poem available at http://www.empowermentresources.com/info2/childrenlearn-long_version.html).

O'Hare, N. (2006) *'All Ears' the things that matter*, National Literacy Trust, London.

Reggio Emilia Infant –Toddler Centres and Pre-schools (2000) 3rd printing *The Hundred Languages of Children, Narrative of the Possible*, Reggio-Emilia, Italy: Reggio Children.

Robson, S (2006) *Developing Thinking and Understanding in Young Children*, Routledge, Oxford.

Scottish Government, Learning and Teaching Scotland (2008) Curriculum for Excellence: Learning at the early level (www.curriculumforexcellencescotland.gov.uk).

Scottish Government, Learning and Teaching Scotland (2010) Pre-Birth to Three Positive Outcomes for Scotland's Children and Families, National Guidance (www.ltlscotland.org.uk).

Steiner Waldorf Schools Fellowship (http://www.steinerwaldorf.org/earlyyears.html).

Welsh Assembly Government, Department for Children, Education, Lifelong Learning and Skills (2008) The Foundation Phase:Framework for Children's Learning for 3 to 7 year-olds in Wales (http://wales.gov.uk/topics/educationandskills/earlyyearshome/foundation_phase/?lang = en).

Tickell, C. (2011) 'The Early Years: Foundations for life, health and learning – An independent report on the Early Years Foundation Stage to Her Majesty's Government', Crown copyright (www.education.gov.uk).

Whitebread,D. (ed) 2nd edition (2003) *Teaching and Learning in the Early Years*, Routledge, London.

Chapter 2

Athey, C. (2007) (2nd edition) *Extending Thought in Young Children: A Parent Teacher Partnership*, Paul Chapman Publishing, London.

Bertram, T. & Pascal, C. (2006) *The Baby Effective Early Learning Programme (BEEL)*, Amber Publishing, Birmingham.

Carr, M. (2001) *Assessment in Early Childhood Settings*, Paul Chapman, London.

References

Csikzenthmihalyi, M. (1979) The Concept of Flow', in *Play and Learning*, (ed.) B.Sutton-Smith, pp 257-74, Gardner Press, New York.

Dowling, M. (2010) *Young Children's Personal, Social and Emotional Development*, Sage, London.

Katz (1995) *Talks with Teachers of young Children*, Ablex Publishing Company, New Jersey USA.

Kline, N. (1999) *Time to Think, Listening to Ignite the Human Mind*, Ward Lock, London.

Laevers, F. (ed) (1994) *The Leuven involvement Scale for Young Children* (manual and video) Experiential Education Series, No.1, Leuven: Centre for Experiential Education.

Laevers, F. (2000) 'Forward to Basics! Deep-level learning and the Experiential Approach', *Early Years*, 20(2):20-9.

Laevers, F., Declerq,B., Marin, C., Moons, J. and Stanton, F. *Observing Involvement in Children From Birth to 6 Years*, Averbode, cego publishers, Belguim.

McClelland, M., Acock, C.,Piccinin, A., Rhea, S.A. and Stallings, M.(2012) 'Relations between preschool attention span-persistence and age 25 educational outcomes', *Early Childhood Research Quarterly*, 28.

Ministry of Education, New Zealand (1996) *Te Whariki: Early Childhood Curriculum*, New Zealand Learning Media Ltd, Auckland.

Moylett, (2011) 'Friendly Places: Learning and Development, Communication Part 2', *Nursery World*.

Pascal, C.,Bertram, A., Ramsden, F. & Saunders, M. (2001) (3rd edn) Effective Early Learning Programme (EEL), University College Worcester: Centre for Research in Early Childhood Education.

Podmore, May & Carr (2001) *Early Childhood Folio*, 5, 6-9.

Robson, S. (2006) *Developing Thinking and Understanding in Young Children*, Routledge, Oxford.

Stewart, N. (2011) *How Children Learn, the characteristics of effective early learning*, Early Education, London.

Chapter 3

Banerjee, P.N. & Tamis-LeMonda C.S. (2007) 'Infants' persistence and mothers' teaching as predictors of toddlers' cognitive development', *Infant Behaviour & Development 30* (2007) 479-491.

Bruce, T. (2001) *Learning through Play: Babies, Toddlers and the Foundation Years*, Hodder & Stoughton, London.

Claxton, G. (2000) *Building Learning Power, Helping Young People Become Better Learners*, TLO Limited, Bristol.

Claxton, G. (2006) Expanding the Capacity to Learn: A new end for education?, British Educational Research Association Annual Conference, Warwick University (06.09.12).

Gerhardt, S. (2004) *Why Love Matters: How affection shapes a baby's brain*, Routledge, London.

Grotberg, E. (1995) A guide to promoting resilience in children: strengthening the human spirit, Early Childhood Development: *Practice and Reflections*, 8, Bernard van Leer Foundation.

High Scope (for more information on the original project and ongoing work see http://www.highscope.org).

Lansbury, J. (2012) 'The infant need experts don't talk about' (http://www.janetlansbury.com/2012/07/the-infant-need-experts-dont-talk-about/).

References

Lehrer, J. (2009) 'DON'T! The secret of self-control', *The New Yorker* (18.05.09).

Murray, L. & Andrews, L. (2000) *The Social Baby*, The Children's Project, Richmond.

Sylva, K., Melhuish, E., Sammons, P., Siraj-Blatchford, I., & Taggart. B. (2012) *Effective Pre-school, Primary and Secondary Education 3-14 Project (EPPSE 3-14) – Final Report from the Key Stage 3 Phase: Influences on Students' Development form age 11-14*, Department for Education.

Schweinhart, L. J., & Weikart, D. P. (1997). *Lasting differences: The HighScope Preschool Curriculum Comparison study through age 23* (Monographs of the HighScope Educational Research Foundation, 12). Ypsilanti, MI: HighScope Press.

'Finn and the welly' (http://www.youtube.com/watch?v =iQqAUfhSzTQ).

Chapter 4

Bransford, J. (ed) (2000) *How People Learn: Expanded Edition: Brain, Mind, Experience and School*, National Academies Press, Georgia, USA.

Deci, E. L., & Ryan, R. M. (1995). 'Human autonomy: The basis for true self-esteem'. In M. Kemis (ed.), *Efficacy, agency, and self-esteem* (31–49), Plenum, New York.

Goleman, D. (1995) *Emotional Intelligence*, Bloomsbury, London.

Gopnik, A., Meltzoff, A. & Kuhl, P. (1999) *How Babies Think*, Phoenix, London.

Katz (1995) *Talks with Teachers of young Children*, Ablex Publishing Company, New Jersey USA.

Lasater, J. (Quoted in http://www.nikkichau.com/2009/12/20/the-pursuit-of-happiness/).

Sendak, M. (1963) *Where the Wild Things Are*, Random House, London.

Stewart, N. (2011) *How Children Learn*, Early Education, London.

Whitebread, D. (2012) *Developmental Psychology and Early Childhood Education*, Sage, London.

Willis, J (2006) *Research-Based Strategies to Ignite Student Learning: Insights from a Neurologist and Classroom Teacher*, Virginia, USA: ASCD Publications.

'Visual cliff' (http://www.youtube.com/watch?v = p6cqNhHrMJA).

Chapter 5

Claxton, G. (2004) 'Learning to Learn: A Key Goal in a 21st Century Curriculum', A discussion paper for the Qualifications and Curriculum Authority November 2004.

Gussin Paley, V. (2004) *A Child's Work*, University of Chicago Press, Chicago.

Hart, S., Dixon, A., Drummond, M. J. & McIntyre, I. (2004) *Learning without Limits*, Open University Press, Maidenhead. Holt, J, (1964) *How Children Fail*. Penguin, London.

Moylett, H. & Stewart, N. (2012) *Understanding the Revised Early Years Foundation Stage*, Early Education, London.

Early Education (2012) *Development Matters*, Early Education, Crown Copyright, London.

Notes

Acknowledgements

My warm thanks to all the many practitioners, parents and children who have contributed to this book in various ways. In particular I would like to thank:

- Norland Nursery, Bath

- Tamworth Early Years Children's Centre, Staffordshire

- Homerton Children's Centre, Cambridge

- Wiggly Jigglers and Jasmine Pasch, Rich Mix, Shoreditch

- Pastures Way Nursery School, Luton

- Carcroft Primary School, Doncaster.

Special thanks to Jessica and Abi and their parents – Sam, Gemma, Catherine and Dave.

Finally, I am grateful to Di Chilvers and Anni McTavish for helping me along the way.